"Business Lessons from Bollywood"

Insights from a Life in Sales

Hindi films provide examples of success and failure, initiative and inertia. How can inspiration gained from scenes on celluloid translate into real life victories? What should aspirants in a sales career do in the face of resistance? This book is an engaging description of real-life situations that can be handled with some reel-life nudges.

Prashant Sawant is a multi-faceted personality who has been a hardcore sales professional with companies like Godrej and Motorola among others. He is an innovator and quick implementer who is now a corporate trainer for sales professionals.

The essence of Prashant's training is to make people fearless in their approach to business, people and society at large.

Business Lessons from Bollywood is Prashant's guidance to equip people for business battlefields and help them approach prospective customers ranging from a common man to CEOs directly, procuring business success and windfall results.

"Business Lessons from Bollywood"

Insights from a Life in Sales

By

Prashant Sawant

VISHWAKARMA
PUBLICATIONS VP ™

Business Lessons from Bollywood
Insights from a Life in Sales

First Edition - September 2015

© Prashant Sawant

ISBN 978-93-83572-55-7

Published by:
Vishwakarma Publications
283, Budhwar Peth, Near City Post,
Pune- 411 002.
Phone No: (020) 24448989 / 20261157
Email: info@vpindia.co.in
Website: www.vpindia.co.in

Cover Design
Abhishek Darekar

Typeset and Layout
Chaitali Nachnekar

Printed at
Repro India Limited, Mumbai

Preface

This is my first book which is going into print. I have written a few others on various subjects but those are lying safely in my laptop. I have written two film scripts keeping specific actors in mind. I have one script which I hope to develop further soon. I wrote this one keeping Amitabh Bachchan and Nana Patekar in mind, both powerhouses of talent in their own right. In this script, I have penned the story of the tussle for power between the Chief Minister (CM) of Maharashtra and the Prime Minister (PM) of India. The CM wants to be PM and the whole script depicts the things that the CM and PM do to fuel their ambitions. After the success of this book, I am confident that the name of Prashant Sawant will be recognized widely and that this will give me an audience with the iconic Bachchan and Patekar. I am also sure that they will like my script and that it will be filmed soon thereafter.

Does this sound improbable? Maybe to some. To them I would say, "Believe and you will get it". This is the mantra of my life and today I am a published author apart from being a successful entrepreneur.

I am nearly halfway through my life journey and have reached a position which I could not have imagined a few decades ago. Let me bore you with a brief flashback.

I was born in Mumbai nearly five decades ago to a simple couple; my father worked for Mahanagar Telephone Nigam Limited or MTNL and my mother was a municipal school teacher. We lived in a chawl in Tardeo and I hardly remember anything about those years of my life except for the violent arguments and subsequent bloody (literally) fights between the poor residents of the chawl over trivial issues such as the order of buckets placed in the queue for water, which only used to come between 8pm and 9pm. I found those evenings very impressive as each resident hurled the choicest of abuses on each other while fighting aggressively. I was about four or five-years-old then. I always say this in my parenting seminars and I don't mind saying this again, a child is very impressionable between the ages of three to eight. Whatever he/ she sees, will remain with him/ her for the rest of his/ her life. Take my example, these events that I witnessed subconsciously became a part of my own behaviour. I would give gaalis, shout at someone when I was angry, get angry at the slightest provocation, and charge towards someone with the intention of killing them, among other things. These instincts remained with me for a long time. Even today, they surface every now and then, though I am consciously trying (I think I have been 80% successful in this) to bury this wild side. My father, a simple but intelligent man (my cousin Sanjay, who is much older than me, had the privilege of being with my father, his mama, for quite a number of years and vouches for the fact that he was an astute man) that he was, must have sensed that the chawl was not a proper environment in which to bring up a child so he bought a flat in Borivali in the 70s. He wanted me away from these dangerous but loving people. These residents were the best of friends as well as the worst of enemies. They operated from the heart and not from the head. All these qualities I retain at my core. Even though I was exposed to the finest of intellectuals, sophisticated, rich and famous people in my later years, if you scratch my surface, you will find those chawl characteristics I was talking about. I feel ashamed of that behaviour sometimes, of the anger, rudeness and ruthless aggression. But that's me and I have made my peace with that side of me now.

Writing has also calmed me down a lot. A person who reads a lot, can write a lot. I don't know why but I was and am a voracious reader. Even after eating bhel puri on a piece of paper, I had the habit of completely reading that piece of paper.

I lost my father when I was barely six and my brother one-year-old. My mother took great pains to bring us up well. She inspired me to make something of my life. I did engineering, worked in various top corporates in India and abroad. Yet every time I go back to that chawl, I feel nostalgic. I feel the presence of my father, my grandfather, my grandmother and my uncle there. Even today, I go there to touch those railings, those stairs, those windows, those walls, thinking that at some point in time, these physical things were touched by all my dear relatives.

After my father expired, I returned to the chawl for a few years. There again, I lived with those rowdy boys. I remember I used to stand at the lassi shop and look at the glass of lassi for hours. I used to not have money but I used to just keep on looking at those glasses like a grown up man in a topless bar. Once a friend of mine from the chawl saw me staring at those glasses and pulled me inside the shop and ordered a lassi. I had that glass of lassi for the first time in my life and I remember wishing that it would never get over—it was so delicious! My friend saw the sadness on my face when the lassi got over and he ordered another glass. When I asked him why he wasn't having any, he said, he hated it. I don't know whether he hated it or whether he just wanted me to have lassi to my heart's content. These were the kinds of people I met there. I met many well-to-do people in my life later on but have not seen someone as generous or as concerned about someone else's pain as the people there. Only a man in pain understands the pain of others and does something to eliminate it.

I lost my father but due to love showered on me by my friend circle, consisting of the middle class society in Borivali, I became an engineer. A man is as good as the company he keeps. I was pushed towards academics and studies because of the friends I made in Borivali who were very focused on making something of their lives. All of them are well placed today—working at very senior positions in corporates, owning their own businesses, or working abroad.

As I said earlier, after I lost my father, my mother went into a state of shock, which I don't think she has recovered from even after 40 years. As a result I did not have much of an upbringing. She never told me not to do this or that. She used to think of me as a child who had lost his father so early and so she let me do whatever gave me happiness. I was growing like a wild tree. The things I learnt while living in Tardeo were imprinted on my mind and they conflicted with the genteel society I witnessed in Borivali. As a result I found myself very confused.

Suddenly, I saw a ray of light.

In those days owning a television (TV) was a luxury. Today in my 1,800 sqft flat, I have a TV in every room but in those days, I used to go to someone else's house, sit on the cold floor and wait for movies to begin every Sunday at 6pm. I started watching movies, and they became my parents. The things heroes did shaped my value system.

Even today, when I think of the typical hero (from the 70s and 80s) of Hindi cinema, I think of the values they endorse, like being honest, loving your parents, taking on unbelievable challenges and thinking positive against extreme odds. These are the things that have brought me to where I am today.

I was always very aggressive in my job, both internally (within the company) as well as externally (in the market). I always behaved correctly, never did anything which put me to shame and chased high, seemingly impossible targets. These qualities have shaped my character.

I liked music a lot. I used to stand next to taxis, just to listen to the songs which were playing on their radios. I used to stand near any shop which used to blare my favorite songs.

During my engineering days, one of my classmates, Jiten Shah, introduced me to the music of Pankaj Udhas and Jagjit Singh and to ghazals in general. I am eternally grateful to him. Another friend, Avinash Chauhan, introduced me to, and described to me in great detail, the nuances of the music of R D Burman. RD (Or "Tublu" as he was known to those close to him) has given me a lot of happiness through his music.

I was on the footboard of a bus travelling back home in Borivali when I saw a man reading a Mid-Day paper whose headline was announcing RD's demise. I took the paper from him, read the headline and went numb. I forgot everything. The bus crossed my designated stop. I got down two stops later and dragged myself back home in utter pain. I'll never forget that moment. Even today when anyone talks highly about RD, my eyes turn moist and there is a lump in my throat. Around the same time, I also remember watching a music show on Zee Marathi titled Sa Re Ga Ma. The show was judged by Pandit Hridaynath Mangeshkar. During the show, Hridaynath made it a point not to mention a word about RD. I believe that when we talk about Indian music, RD has to be mentioned or else the discussion is incomplete. Maybe Mangeshkar was angry with RD, because of Asha's marriage to him. Whatever the case, I was furious. Though I like Hridaynath, who is a great music composer in his own right, I was terribly hurt by his indifferent attitude.

So coming back to my story, I was brought up on a staple diet of Hindi movies. I was particularly crazy about Amitabh Bachchan. He was and is God to me. His onscreen persona and his conduct in real life is awesome. I try to behave like him (as he is in real life) in my own dealings with other people but I end up behaving like the characters he played instead (in his reel life).

But the things which I have learnt from him in movies like Trishul, Deewar and Sholay, I will remember for the rest of my life. I feel these movies should be part of the curriculum in schools. Though the real credit must got to Salim saab and Javed saab for creating such master pieces. If both these scriptwriting geniuses had stayed together, we may have got the chance to watch many more such masterpieces. I have read several books that attempt to pinpoint the reason for the split but none of them provide a direct answer. I am still clueless. It appears that even Salim saab doesn't know why the separation took place as has been revealed in his biography.

I have worked in various corporates, American companies, Japanese companies, companies from the Gulf region, and of course, Indian companies. I have used the principles for success taught by Amitabh in his movies at various stages in my corporate life and I have emerged triumphant.

Currently, I give lectures and conduct workshops in various corporates and schools of business management. I conduct "Bollywood satsangs" where I discuss movies like Sholay, etc. and what the corporate world can learn from them. My lectures/ workshops borrow wisdom from Bollywood, especially from the scripts written by Salim-Javed.

People get mesmerized when I provide anecdotes from Hindi movies to illustrate my point and make it clear.

Sometimes I have taken seminars that stretch for more than three hours. After the seminar, a few participants come and tell me that they didn't even attend nature's call as they didn't want to miss any of my Bollywood pearls of wisdom.

This set me thinking and I decided to pen these Bollywood gems into a book through which I hope to help a lot of professionals who are struggling with difficult business problems.

I watch at least one of these three movies—Deewar, Sholay or Trishul—every Saturday, to draw inspiration from them. I must have seen these movies a countless number of times, but every time, without fail, I learn something new. They also gave me solutions to everyday problems, which I used to go through in my personal or professional life at that point in time and even today. I am indebted to the Indian film industry and this is my humble tribute to it.

Enjoy the roller coaster ride! Happy reading!

❑❑❑

Table of Contents

Be a good person to become a good salesperson 1

Subconscious Mind... 12

Positive thinking Vs Positive believing 24

Achieve new milestones and create records 36

First Impressions: Appearance and Body Language 48

Knowing your Customer: Separating the Potentials
from the Bloodsuckers 62

Internal customer, external customer and growth 75

The Golden Formula :: 70:20:10 88

Getting an Appointment *101*

*Is Sales an Art or a Science? The Law of Averages (LOA)
and Listening* *114*

Under commit, over perform *128*

Growth Parameters *140*

"Be a good person to become a good salesperson"

Most people tend to avoid salespeople. Why is this? The general perception about the salesperson is that he/ she is smart and witty, with a silver tongue but is also very cunning and out to sell whatever he has, with scant respect for the need/ requirement of the buyer.

Such an opportunistic attitude is best described through a dialogue of Salman Khan which goes as follows: *"Apna kaam banta toh bhaad mein gayee janata"*. This translates to: if my work gets completed, then I don't care if all of humanity goes to hell.

Some salespersons are pushy, hence people tend to avoid them. Pushing somebody to do your bidding is selfish. In any relationship, if we put our self before the other person that relationship is doomed to have an expiry date.

What is the spelling of the word business? Would you rather that it was spelt bisuness? The first spelling—business—is correct. If you observe the word closely, you realise that the alphabet "u" comes before "i". What does this signify? That in business we always need to put "u" or "the customer", before "i" or "yourself" and your selfish interests. This is when business will take place.

Many words are spelt in such a manner that that their meaning becomes apparent. Consider the following words:

Stop - if you don't stop, you will reach top.

Close - If you take "c" out of the word, you "lose". This means that in any business situation, the business ultimately should culminate into payment for the product/ service being provided. When the seller doesn't get the "c" i.e. cash/ cheque, he loses the deal.

Trust - The most important component in any relationship in this world is trust. Whether the relationship is business oriented or a personal relationship, trust is an irreplaceable entity. It is like the salt in your food, without which your food would be tasteless. Why it spelt t-r-u-s-t? In any business relationship, the most important thing is "time". The time by which you reach after taking/ giving an appointment, the time by which you deliver a product/ service as against the time you had promised, etc. Hence the "t" in trust stands for time. When you don't meet your time commitments, the "t" gets removed from the word trust. What remains is rust. Thus the relationship rusts when time commitments are not adhered to.

In the movie, Trishul, Amitabh Bachchan's character Vijay, commits to R K Gupta (played by Sanjeev Kumar) to buy his land. Vijay promises to make the payment within 15 days. Mind you, in his own mind, Vijay knows that he will be able to pay Gupta in 6-7 days but he still asks for 15 days. I would say his mental calculation was as follows: On day zero (the same day on which he meets Gupta) he will go to Madho Singh, the gounda who has illegally occupied Gupta's (now Vijay's) land and ask him to vacate the land tomorrow i.e. on day one. Vijay knows that, if Madho Singh doesn't comply, he will fight with him & his goons and throw them out. On day two, he will go to Prem Chopra, the money lender, mortgage the land documents and collect Rs. 5 lakh. On the same day or may be the next day, i.e. day three, he will go to Gupta's office to pay him. So Vijay has mentally calculated three days but promised 15 days. In the movie, he delivers the cheque on the seventh day. Now why did three days get stretched to seven? May be this time lag happened because Prem Chopra was not available immediately or he may have taken a few days to arrange for such a large sum of money (Rs. 5 lakh was a very big sum in 1978. Just to put things in perspective, the price of 10 gms of gold was Rs. 685 in 1978).

The pushy sales guys have various barriers to the successful completion of business. They seem to be deaf to what the client has to say. They just want to hear the word *"yes"* from their client and will bother him so much that in the end, he agrees and says, "Even if I don't need this product, what I really need now is chootkara (freedom) from this parasite". Generally when people buy a product, they don't buy the product, they buy the benefits of that product, meaning they buy what that product is going to do for them. In the case of a client being hounded by a pushy salesperson, getting the salesman out of his hair seems to be the sole benefit of the product to the customer.

Sometimes children who beg on the road just refuse to take "no" for an answer and keep on following you until you give them something. They will touch you, pull your dress, even touch your feet or put their head on your feet. I have seen young college girls getting targeted for this royal treatment. These 17-something young girls give a few coins to these street urchins and buy the benefit of a peace of mind.

Some salespeople are "chipku", they stick to you like Fevicol till you get rid of them by giving them the sale. Some salespeople are so dominating that they literally force you to give them the sale.

The above descriptions are the very reason for the general public to avoid them like "plague".

When you push for a sale, you sometimes know that under normal circumstances, this person will not buy this product because he does not need it or he is short of cash. By pushing him you are spoiling the name of the salesperson community. This may be one of the reasons why I "unfairly" compared these kinds of salespeople to the street children who have little choice and need to beg to keep their bodies and souls together.

There are two types of sales. One is "Push", which is universal and employed by all and sundry. The other one is "Pull". Most salespeople employ the strategy of "push" as that is easiest. Most buyers are decent individuals and can't be rude to pushy salespeople for too long; even if they don't require the product, they end up buying it, as I mentioned earlier. Now this is a very short term strategy as this person will run away from this type of sales guy and the sales guy may not be able to get any further business from him. Whenever the sales guy approaches him again, the buyer will say that he has already bought his product only and I repeat *"Only because you wanted me to buy it"*. In his mind he says, *"I have bought this only because I wanted to save my relationship with you"* (he may be a relative, friend, friend of a friend's colleague, etc. of the sales guy) and not because he actually wanted it. So the bottom line here is, the buyer feels he has already helped the salesperson, you, once at the cost of his own interests but does not intend to repeat this forever. The easiest sales is that which takes place through existing customers who want to buy from you again. If a customer has bought something from you and whatever he has bought, he did because he wanted it, because that product was offering benefits which he desperately needed, he will most probably repeat his purchases from you. He has benefitted from you once and wants to benefit again and again. In the first example, he can't make you benefit when he clearly stands to lose from the transaction.

Let me give you another small example. People buy life insurance-related products for a minimum of five times in their life. First when they get their first job, second when they stop being happy, i.e. get married (I am just joking. I have seen many people who began to feel happy only after they were married. The prime example of such a person is "me"), third when they become a father for the first time, fourth when they become a father again and fifth when they think of their retirement. A well-known life insurance company in India, where I am associated, has 30 crore customers. Going by the above mentioned logic, how many policies should this company have sold? The answer is a 150 crore policies should have been in their kitty. Sadly, they only had 38 crore policies. Even 38 crore is a staggering figure as there are several countries like Singapore, whose entire population is smaller than this figure. However, this low figure (compared to the number of customers) is only because most of the sales has happened through pushing. The product is not sold as a benefit here but it is sold as a favor to the person who is selling it. This kind of *"I win, you lose"* scenario, can never yield good results.

I am going to stick my neck out and say that if you are in retail business and if you have even ten loyal customers (customers who feel that you are a seller who puts the buyer's interest before your own), you will become a roaring success and you will have more customers in your portfolio than you can manage, sooner than you can imagine.

In life, the only situation which you must strive to achieve is a "win-win" situation. It is the most rewarding and profitable relationship for both the seller and the buyer. Most of the time salespeople are brought up with the ill-conceived notion that for the seller to win, the buyer has to lose. This is a win-lose relationship—I win and you lose. This can never be a long-term relationship. Another type of relationship which is short-lived is when you sell your product at a loss so that the customer benefits for the time being and you think that you will recover the loss later. This is an 'I lose, you win' relationship and will not last more than a few days.

A salesperson needs to be a good person. A good person doesn't need to try to be a good salesperson. Any sales will automatically gravitate towards you because of your goodness.

Any sale that takes place anywhere on planet Earth follows three logical steps. Three things are sold, necessarily in the order that I am about to outline. The product gets sold last. First the salesperson sells himself, then the organization who is promoting the product gets sold and last but not the least, the product finds its rightful place in the mind of the customer and then finds its place in his home.

So when you see a good person, it is obvious that the customer will buy him instantaneously and then his sale becomes a cake walk as the customer is convinced about the quality (honesty, knowledge, attitude, etc.) of the salesperson and tends to equate the salesperson's quality with the organization's or product's quality.

Connect → Convey → Convince (3 stages of sales)

Once a sage asked his shishya, *"What is the difference between God and Good?"* Shishya could not answer. The answer, the sage gave, was *"zero"*. Saying this, he demonstrated what he meant by making a circle with his index finger and thumb. *"Hence anyone who is good, is God"* he added. When we look at a small child, we feel we are watching "God in action". The child doesn't have any ill feelings about anybody, be it a person or a situation, among other things. When we throw a small child up in the air, he is delirious with joy and he smiles and laughs. For arguments sake, let us say that you try to do this with a grown up man, what do you think will happen? He will be scared to death. Why is he scared? He probably feels that the man below will not catch him. Why does the man feel like this? The same man, in his own life, may have cheated a few people by betraying them be it his friend, family or wife. When he has done something like this, he may expect others to do the same with him. We live in a society built on "mistrust." We always expect people to do their worst to us. On the contrary, a child has never betrayed anyone's trust and hence doesn't even know the meaning of "dhokha" or deceit yet.

Being a good person requires lot of control and discipline because you need to be honest with your own self and also with the customer. You need to first understand his needs and give him a solution which you would have given to yourself if you were in a similar situation. Hats off to those kinds of professionals! They will no longer be called salespeople. The world will salute them and stand on its head to please professionals like these. On the contrary, being good takes a lot of hard work and is not an easy choice to make. It is too much of an effort for a negative and dishonest person. In this case, there will come a moment in his/ her transaction with a client; a small window when he/ she will let his/ her guard down. Such a salesperson's eyes will blurt out the truth (that he/ she wants to win at any cost, at any negative cost to the buyer) and he/ she will be out of the sale.

What I am trying to say is that selling is treated by some crooks who are a blemish to the profession of sales as cheating. When we lie about the capabilities of a product we are selling, we are actually cheating our customer. Like when someone dives deep in a swimming pool and shits (I hope you have never actually tried to do this); his shit will inevitably float to the surface. Similarly, truth always catches up with a person who lies and will eventually destroy his/ her relationship with his/ her client. Even if we make a sale by cheating, be sure that God has seen this transaction and you will to have to pay for your dishonesty in this birth, without exception. We reap, what we sow.

Some people ask, why they should be honest in their transactions when most of the people they have met have cheated them. If you have been cheated, you have allowed the other person to cheat you. Nobody can cheat you unless you place your trust in them. When you place your trust in someone without taking the necessary precautions such as checking up on their credibility, it is entirely your fault not theirs. Being cheated does not justify becoming a cheater. Like in Indian law, if the glass window of your car is not closed properly and your valuables get stolen, you are at fault and the law will catch you for abetting the crime. Like in the older version of the movie Dostana starring Amitabh Bachchan and Zeenat Aman, when Zeenat walks on to a road wearing a short dress, Amitabh scolds her for the tamasha which takes place when some roadside gundas begin to tease her.

A career in sales is all about building relationships. This is true of our lives in general. If you had to choose between having ten lakhs in a bank and ten friends who will do anything for you, which would you choose? In sales, if we build relationships, it has a cascading effect. These relationships will be responsible for further introductions to new clients with minimum effort on your part. Otherwise you need to search for and convince new prospects every single time.

Once upon a time, a neta or politician, refused to fight elections from a particular constituency saying that all the people in that area knew him. His competitor wanted to fight elections from the same area for the same reason, i.e. all the people knew him. One of them knew, people disliked him while the other knew that his constituency trusted and respected him. The neta who wanted to run away was a crook and the people knew it, whereas the other neta was a gem and the people knew that too. Who do you think was victorious? For how long would the crooked neta be able to move to a new constituency?

Being a good person has its own rewards. If you have been pursuing a sale for a long time and you end up losing it, you may feel dejected for a few days but I want to say that have patience, God will compensate you for your efforts. You may find that you get the sale without much of an effort after a few days or months or you may find that the client you were chasing turned out to be a cheat himself. Patience is the key!

In the film Deewar, Shashi Kapoor happens to get a job at a department store just when he is about to lose hope in his desperate search for a job. His happiness is short-lived because in a few seconds, the person who is supposed to join that day comes panting and says he was late because he didn't have money for the bus ticket (though personally, I consider this to be an excuse as he could have done whatever was supposed to be done to take care of such a situation, earlier). Shashi then refuses the job on some minor pretext so that the man who is in desperate need of money gets the job. Shashi (once again) remains jobless but God is watching this from above. To give employment to the needy man was God's job, which Shashi does by being selfless, hence God is touched and feels obliged to help Shashi in some way. The benefits that Shashi receives are manifold as in the movie he goes on to become a police inspector, which ultimately makes him famous. If you help someone with Rs 1, God will give you more than Rs 1,000. If you cheat someone of Rs 1, God will make sure you lose Rs 1. Seems like a small amount but there is a rider attached to this; while that Rs 1 goes from you, it will give you some pain, both physical and emotional, while passing. Hence stay away from robbing people of their possessions.

Projecting your products in a misleading manner so as to

benefit from the sales commission follows the same rules that I have stated above, so be careful. I mean it and this is the gospel truth.

The organisation which is, the biggest and most trusted financial services brand in the insurance industry has many products, which in this case are policies for customers. When I ask the agents (who sell policies in India) what their best insurance policy is, some name a few of the policies, some say that the best policy is decided on the basis of the need and the requirements of the customer, which is quite true. However, I always tell them that "Honesty is the best policy". I tell them that if they are honest, they will get all that they want in life and in business or in any sphere of their lives. As salespeople, these agents are aware of all the strengths and weaknesses of their products. When they meet a customer who is confused about what to purchase and is depending on them for advice, they are in a position to exploit the situation, which is what I mean when I tell them to be honest. They need to be honest & give right solution to the customers for their benefits.

In a nutshell, this chapter talks about how one must not try too hard to become a rocking salesperson but focus more on being a good person. It is easier said than done as cheating someone is much easier than conducting our sales career/ business career/ life in general, in an honest and truthful manner. If you strive to be good, God will give you the strength necessary to be the best human being around.

Happy honest selling!

□□□

"Subconscious Mind"

In the beginning of the film "Om Shanti Om", Shah Rukh Khan plays the role of a fatherless, struggling actor with a funny-sounding surname, a filmy, loud mother, a home which is more like a hut, a poor friend and he only gets the roles of extras in films, with no dialogues. His list of misfortunes is endless. However, he has one thing which only one percent of humanity has and that is the positive visualization method which even he is blissfully unaware of.

Though poor, he dreams of a having a Kapoor surname (instead of Makhija), a big bungalow, a round bed (as in Yash Chopra's movies), a silk gown (as the actor Rajkumar used to wear), around 50 servants, a fleet of cars, servants sliding chappals on his feet before he places them on the floor, when he wakes up in the morning and gets out of bed, another servant holding a glass of juice for him to drink as soon as he wakes up, etc. He dreams about this endlessly. After this, owing to a sinister twist in the plot, he gets killed in an accident. His soul departs his body and immediately enters the body of a baby, as yet unborn, of the superstar "Kapoor". This is how he eventually gets everything that he dreamt of in his last birth. Even though he dies, his positive visualization comes true. He is given one more birth to make sure all his positive visualizations are brought to reality.

This scene speaks volumes about the power of the subconscious mind. Whatever we visualize with passion, whatever we believe with complete conviction, often comes true.

Now that you think about it, success is actually so easy to achieve and yet so difficult. "Easy" because if you think about a positive outcome of your task, visualize it in as minute detail as possible, feel the happiness/ satisfaction which you would feel at being successful, then you will be successful.

The only catch here is that visualization sometimes does not work. It has to be accompanied by a few other things. The subconscious mind understands only two things—images and emotions.

Whenever you visualize something, you have to associate that picture in your mind with the right emotions. You have to feel the emotions which you would feel when you "get" whatever you have visualized or you "become" whatever you have visualized.

If your body feels (emotions) the outcome, you get whatever you have visualized. This is true 100 percent of the times.

Why is this difficult? That's because we cannot bring ourselves to the point where we believe a positive outcome, we cannot bring ourselves to the point of feeling the desired outcome when our current situation is pulling us back in the pit.

The future should be guided by our desires for the future

not by our regrets of the past. The few who can think of the unthinkable and believe in it, will get it.

Belief is a word used by many writers but nobody talks about how to build belief. Part of the spelling of the word belief contains the word LIE. In a sense you actually have to lie to yourself and tell yourself that no matter how horrible your current situation may be, you will reach for the sky one day and be successful.

We have two types of minds—conscious and subconscious. Our conscious mind is active 10 percent of the time while our subconscious is active 90 percent of the time.

We barely use our conscious mind (not even 25 percent of its capability is fully utilized) and we keep our subconscious virtually unused. Most of the time, we use our subconscious mind against ourselves as we expect a negative outcome from most situations and we get, what we "expect" not what we "want".

It is like God has given us Rs 100 and we have used only five to six rupees. We surrender the balance Rs 95 to God saying we have not used it.

Most people are not to be blamed for this under-utilization of their subconscious as nobody teaches them how to use it to their benefit. The Conscious mind understands logic and reason whereas the subconscious understands only images and emotions. If you hold the picture (Image) of what you want in your mind and feel the happiness (emotion) which you would feel on achieving what you are expected to achieve, you will most certainly get what you want.

When the Wright brothers first talked about a metal box flying in air and carrying people with it (invention of the modern aeroplane), people thought they were doing black magic and cheating innocent members of the public. But when actually they flew their plane, people thought that it was a miracle. People understood later that it was neither black magic nor a miracle when they came to know about the science behind it.

In the same way, today if you achieve something with the help of your subconscious mind, you feel that it is a miracle but you will not call it a miracle (instead you will call it pure science), when you understand how it works.

The subconscious is a lethal weapon and can give you anything you want or can make you anything you want to be. Our parents, teachers and religious gurus teach us how to use these lethal weapons against ourselves.

Don't get shocked, I will explain. It is extremely painful when all these respected individuals who play important roles in our lives actually end up wrecking our lives. They even think that they are actually helping us. This is such a tragedy!

When we are small, we don't have many negative emotions. These emotions are introduced to us by our Gods, i.e. our mother and father. Though they are our well-wishers, unfortunately they are also ignorant about the venom they are putting in the mind of their vulnerable child; a poison which is going to slowly ruin his/ her entire life.

The first 2,000 days of any child's life are very important. The child has many brain cells that die or wither away if not exercised in the right way. It is for this reason why preschool, nursery and daycare centres are important institutions for a child. It is sad that the importance of these institutions is often not realized by people in powerful places.

Just imagine, a child has the ability to pick up any language within the first 700 days of his/ her entry in this world. And we take them to be fools. If they are taught things at that stage, they could be champions. They should be given the right attitude. They don't know the emotion of fear. However when a mother warns her child not to do something, like climb a tree, when she says, *"Don't climb, you will fall"* (utter negative non sense), she plants the seeds of doubt in him. It's possible that the child may fall but there is no reason why you have to scare him from trying something adventurous. He becomes timid, doesn't try anything aggressive when grown up and then the same mom will ridicule him for his timidness. Who is the real culprit? Parents use fear to control their children. They don't have the time and patience to control their child's exuberance hence they resort to using fear tactics which causes lasting damage on the child. This fearful attitude remains with the child till the time he doesn't need parental supervision, i.e. when he becomes a man. The grip of fear remains with him and prevents him from being successful. Fear and success can never coexist like fire and ice can't coexist; one of them has to give way.

Therefore, while target setting is done by your conscious mind, achieving success is dependent on how much you trust your subconscious mind.

The havoc that teachers and religious gurus play in our lives

After our parents, it's the role of the teacher to mould the way a child loses faith in their subconscious mind. The following sloka is known by most young children who go to school:

> *Gurur Brahma, Gurur Vishnu,*
> *Gurur Devo Maheshwaraha,*
> *Gurur Sakshat Parabrahma*
> *Tasmai Sri Gurave Namaha*

The community of teachers to which this hymn is addressed is non-existent now. The education system is filled with parikhsharthies (exam seekers) instead of vidyaarthies (knowledge seekers). Who's responsible for this big change? I believe the teachers are the culprits.

There exist individuals who take private tuition classes for which they charge you a heavy sum. In return they allow you to bunk classes in school and you still get your attendance. They are obviously greasing the palms of college authorities to look the other way when students bunk class. They're creating a system of inefficiency in which they achieve maximum benefit. The student still has to attend their classes, the student has to pay fees for both the college and the tuition centre, the tuition teacher asks students to bunk classes because anyway the college virtually teaches nothing and they pay bribes to college officials for the non-performance of their duties of teaching and insisting on student attendance. The system sucks.

These are the values put forward by modern day teachers. A guru or teacher, is the one who takes you from gu (darkness) to ru (light). Today the exact reverse is taking place and nobody seems to mind it at all.

In one of his movies, Sanjay Dutt says, *"I am a crook because of Mr Amitabh Bachchan. Because on TV he keeps saying "Con banega carorepati," hence I am a CON".* Sadly this is true in today's times. If you are not a CON, people will ask you, *"Aap hain KAUN?"*

Teachers tell students in school that if you don't study, you will fail. This is NEGATIVE. This is where teachers introduce us to the fear of failing.

Next in line are our religious gurus. They are all frauds with very few exceptions. In my opinion, religion is biggest and best business in the market today. Religious gurus are the biggest, most unethical salesmen on Earth. They will check your KUNDALI (horoscope) and tell you five good things—the same general things are told to all and sundry. Check Bejan Daruwala's horoscope predictions if you don't believe me. Read them as you would a comic book. Keep all the predictions of the last six months with you and you will know how he only churns out these predictions with no real insight. Bejan also involves Lord Ganesha in his con act, so that you take him seriously and will believe him for the fear of Lord Ganesha because his catchphrase is: Ganesha says. I don't know what he means by Ganesha says. Did Ganesha come and shout in his ears? Does Ganesha do this every day? Why does Ganesha do this? To feed professionals like Bejan? These questions are best left unanswered. Now these con men have told you a few good things and won your trust (a perfect selling trick). People should trust themselves as God resides in all of us. But the sad truth is that we do trust outside forces more than the life force which is throbbing inside all of us. Then they show you fear. You panic and ask for a solution (again a perfect selling principal of converting a need into an impulse to buy a solution. Here the need is imaginary as the fear has been created by this thief baba). The baba says there is a solution and asks you to spend an amount of Rs X as dakhina (the swamy's fees) and perform a pooja ceremony. I have a personal friend whom I will not name as I don't want him to get into trouble, who tells me how these so called poojaries actually cheat people. Most of the time these poojaries are also "hawas" ke poojari. They take undue advantage of ladies and young girls by claiming sexual favours in return for exerting their 'power' to solve their problems. Such things rarely come out into the public domain as the victims feel threatened and worry that God will be angry with them if they complain. Most of the time when the eyes of the ladies open, it is too late as they cannot make a public statement because society will end up punishing them only. Few such cases have come out, but nothing has been done about it by the administration.

The business of religion runs on inducing a fear psychosis in the masses. If God has to come and stay with us for a few days, most people will start complaining about Him being at their homes and not contributing to the monthly budget and occupying expensive sq ft of their space. I am saying this because most people treat their parents (who in my opinion are the biggest and greatest Gods that any of us can ask for) very shabbily. I have seen one of my closest relatives cursing his father in front of me and saying, *"Why doesn't he die? Then I will be able to call my friends home and do things for my happiness which this old man has blocked by staying in my flat"* The old man's bed was kept in the hall. He used to go to the toilet every now and then in torn and shabby clothes and his shameless son used to feel repulsed by the sight and openly pray for his death. One fine day, the old man died and his son shamelessly took all his wealth and lived happily ever after. This to me is evidence that we live in kalyug.

God bless the old man!

Please love your parents to overcome any and every difficulty in your life. The blessings of your parents are like weapons which will never fail when you are faced with some of the biggest calamities in your life.

Loving your parents is similar to praying to God.

What happens when we pray?

Praying is considered to be a way to ask the almighty for whatever you want from life. However I believe that praying is not about asking, it is much more. Let me explain what praying means to me by telling you a small story. It goes like this:

There was a man who died at the ripe old age of 85 and went to heaven. There he met God and after being awestruck at meeting the God in person, he requested God to show him around heaven. God readily accepted his request and asked him to follow him. God took him around various places. After a few strolls, they come across a very large workroom filled with numerous workers. This man was trying to figure out the rationale behind such a workforce. God, sensing his curiosity explained, *"This is a receiving station where we collect*

Subconscious Mind ‖

all applications/ requests sent to me." The man looked around and found that all the men were working with a feverish pace and were immersed up to their neck, in work. They were sorting through huge quantities of paper sheets received from across the globe.

Then God took the man further ahead where again he saw a similar workroom; similar in terms of the number of workers and similar in terms of the workload. God explained, *"This is the delivery section where the blessings people ask for are processed and delivered to the living person who has asked for them."* This section was also working at a feverish speed as so many requests (prayers) to God had to be processed and delivered to people on planet Earth.

They walked further ahead and after a long walk (as the earlier two rooms were mammoth sized) they found a very small room. To the man's great astonishment, this room contained only one man, sitting with an expression of intense boredom on his face. He was doing precious nothing. In the film Shakti, directed by the Great Ramesh Sippy, Amitabh says, *"Jo log kuch nahin karte, who kamaal karte hai."* People who don't do anything create magic. But this man didn't look he was capable of any kamaal or magic. He was sitting idle with his back resting against a worn-out chair and was looking at some far away object with utter disinterest.

The man looked at God with questioning eyes. God said, *"This is the acknowledgment section".* The man asked, *"Why is there only one person handling the entire department?"* Now God looked embarrassed and he said *"After people receive positive answers to their prayers, very few send back acknowledgements. It's very sad but painfully true".*

Now the man was puzzled. His questions were not answered to his satisfaction. He said, "But how does one send acknowledgements to God? To which God replied, *"Just by saying, thank you".*

When we get up in the morning, the first thing we should do is express our gratitude to God. Say, *"Thank you"* to him for still being alive, healthy, having a roof over your head, having a bed to sleep on, etc.

To have gratitude is to be rich and to complain is, to be poor

One of the ways of getting unbelievable results from your powerful subconscious mind is to express gratitude at every step in your life. You will find that the more gratitude you have, the more reasons you will have to be grateful. Unfortunately the reverse of this situation can also manifest itself when you complain. You make your life a series of complaints and nothing moves towards successful completion.

Most failures in life are people who are perpetually in the past and cursing everyone and everything under the sun (except themselves), for their current pathetic (financially, physically, socially and spiritually) state of life.

People who are successful in their lives, have the guts to take responsibility for their fate. Most people who blame everyone else except themselves can never go up as they have not understood the real reasons for their lack of success and that is *"themselves".*

If you want to see the person who is preventing you from achieving whatever you have set your mind on, please go to the mirror and have a look.

The biggest obstacle in your life is YOU.

Take the bull by its balls (Horn is so passé. It would have been used if I was telling this story in 1857. Today we are in 2015) and achieve whatever you want.

The poet Mirza Ghalib wrote a beautiful couplet on this topic, which goes as follows: *"Umre bhar mein yahi galti karta raha, dhool chehre pe lagi thi, aaina saaf krata raha"*. This translates to, *"My entire life I made the mistake of cleaning my mirror because I thought it was dirty when the actual dirt was on my own face"*. What a profound message!

So go and clean your "face" and "face" the world with complete belief in yourself. Your belief will be answered.

I raise a toast to your success!

❏❏❏

Positive thinking Vs Positive believing

When someone talks about positive thinking what do they mean? A person is either happy or sad, you can't be both. Positive thinking is to think in a manner that reflects all the positive things in your life. To have such an attitude is easier said than done (Oops! That's a negative thought).

Positive thinking, as the word suggests, is to think about positive things—positive events, positive outcomes, positive people and the things they have said to you, among other things. This however is not my point. It's great if you can think about positive things but if you want to attract those things in your life, you need to believe that you have received them already or that you have become what you wanted very badly to become. Belief, is the key. Believing makes everything rush towards you in a turbo-charged fashion.

Believing that the outcome is going to be a hundred percent positive, fills you with positive emotions such as elation and happiness. Positive things get attracted to us only through our subconscious mind and the subconscious mind only believes in images and emotions. So we have to believe, we have to create a mental picture of the outcome we want to achieve and above all, we have be aware of the feeling of accomplishment when we undertake any task. This way, the things that we badly want will start moving towards you.

In the movie No Entry, the hero keeps on saying, *"Be positive, be positive"*. Once someone asks him about his blood group and he says, *"B +ve"*. The person who asks him gets irritated at first and later realizes that his blood group actually is "B +ve".

Jokes apart, first let us discuss what positive thinking is and then, what positive believing is. After this we will consider why positive believing is a better proposition when it comes to your overall success in any venture.

By positive and negative thinking I mean the way that we, as humans, worry about events in our future.

When you imagine that what you are going to encounter in the next few minutes, hours or days, is going to turn out in your favor, exactly the way you want it to happen, you're thinking positively. Negative thinking is the opposite of this.

Most people find that their first thoughts when faced with a challenge, are negative.

We are born positive thinkers. As children don't bother about the outcome or impact of their actions (whether positive or negative) on their lives. As we grow older, we also face a few disappointments, failures, etc. along the way as well as the same amount of successes but we tend to remember the negative or disappointing events with more clarity as they leave a lasting impact on us. We simply take whatever we have, as granted and don't value it. If something goes wrong, we get up and brood over that negative event till eternity.

As they say in the world of journalism — good news is no news. Likewise, we don't thank God for what we have, we only go and complain to him about what we don't have or what we want to have. We pester God wherever he resides, be it in temples, masjids or churches.

Every day before you go to sleep, you should physically write down all the things you are grateful for. When we write, our emotional window opens and positive feelings flow into us, guiding us to success.

When you write, you feel different. Try locking yourself into a room, taking a piece of blank paper and writing your goals on it, slowly, one by one; the entire experience will be surreal. Write down each goal as though you are receiving it at that very moment, i.e., believe in it, live it, be positive about it. If you write your goals in this manner, with emotional attachment, in the present tense, being conscious of the moment at which you receive it, it does wonders to your self-esteem and your ability to succeed.

If you were to help someone and he forgets to thank you, how do you feel? Furthermore, for some reason, he comes back only to blame and blackmail you because he feels cheated somehow and wants to set you right, how you would feel? Stop reading for a moment and close your eyes. Think about what you just read. Imagine a friend doing this to you and imagine your feelings at that moment.

God feels the same way when we crib to him and don't thank

him at all. Abhishek Bachchan once visited a religious place and on the way back he was asked what he prayed for. He said he just thanked God for whatever he had been given without even asking for anything.

The following story will elaborate the repercussions of both positive and negative thinking:

Rajan applied for a new job, but his self-esteem was low; his mind was clouded with negative thoughts. He considered himself a failure and unworthy of success. He was sure that he was not going to get the job. He had a negative attitude towards himself, and believed that the other applicants were better and more qualified. Rajan manifested this attitude due to past experiences that left him with a negative impression of job interviews.

His mind was filled with fears concerning the job for an entire week before the actual interview. He was certain he would be rejected. On the day of the interview, he got up late and to his horror he discovered that the shirt he had planned to wear was dirty, and the other one needed ironing. As it was already very late, he went out wearing a shirt full of wrinkles.

During the interview he was tense, nervous, worried about his shirt and hungry because in his hurry to leave he had not had time to eat breakfast. All this distracted his mind and made it difficult for him to focus on the interview. His overall behavior made a bad impression, and consequently he materialized his fear and did not get the job.

Sanjay applied for the same job too, but approached the matter in a different way. He was sure that he was going to get the job.

During the week preceding the interview he often visualized himself making a good impression and getting the job.

In the evening before the interview he prepared the clothes he was going to wear, and went to sleep a little earlier. On day of the interview he woke up earlier than usual, and had ample time to eat breakfast, and then to arrive to the interview before the scheduled time.

He got the job because he made a good impression. He had also of course, the proper qualifications for the job, but so had Rajan.

What do we learn from these two stories? Did Sanjay use any magic to achieve his goal? No, it was all natural. When a person's attitude is positive, they entertain pleasant feelings and constructive images, and visualise what they really want to happen. This brings a sparkle to their eyes, more energy and happiness. Your whole being broadcasts good will, happiness and success. Even your health is affected in a beneficial way. When you walk tall and your voice sounds powerful, your body language reflects the way you feel inside.

Our body cannot differentiate between real and imaginary things. When we believe that we are receiving what we asked for then we get what we ask for.

Imagine yourself standing on the edge of the terrace of the tallest building on the Earth, the Burj Khalifa in Dubai. Close your eyes and imagine this. Or imagine yourself standing on top of a four storey building, maybe where you currently stay. Close your eyes and imagine with all your being. You will feel, you are at the edge of that building. You may feel tense and stressed. Your palms may start to sweat and you may be close to having a nervous breakdown. All this happens because the body cannot understand the difference between the real and the imaginary.

In a Bollywood film, we get a staple diet of love, love songs, fights, blind sisters, old mothers, gajar ka halwa, tragedy, etc. We laugh with the actors, we mentally fight with them (I have seen people actually coaxing the hero on the screen by saying, *"maar, maar saale ko, daat tod saale ka"*) and cry with them, even though we know all this is just make believe and not true.

I read about an experiment conducted on three groups of sportsmen once. One group practiced football for 30 minutes a day. The second group was idle and were left to do whatever they pleased to. The third group was asked to close their eyes and play football in their mind for 30 minutes every day. A few days later, a match was conducted. The group which was not practicing and was left on its own gave bad performances on the field. The groups who actually practiced and the group which practiced in their mind, gave identical performances. That is the power of the mind.

A scene from Deewar

Amitabh goes to Madan Puri and tips him off about when and where his adversary's (Iftekar's) next gold shipment is going to reach the city. Puri promises him a cut from the shipment. When Puri actually receives the gold, instead of paying Amitabh his promised cut, he says, *"Sona toh mujhe mil gaya. Agar ab mein tumhe paise nahi doo toh?"* (Now that I have got my gold, what would you do if I didn't pay you?) Amitabh then says he can't cheat him as he knew the locations of many more such consignments which no one but he can inform Puri about. Realising the long-term prospect of the whole thing, Puri retreats and says, *"Mein toh mazak kar raha tha"* (I was just joking) to which Amitabh says, *"Mein janata tha aap mazak kar rahe the"* (I knew you were joking). This is one example of how to think positive while being good humoured and absolutely confident.

In the scene mentioned above, Amitabh's character shows a lot of positive believing. He believes in his plan, he believes that the plan will meet with success and he very calmly sits with the villain when the villain's own men go to shift the gold (smuggled gold) from the sea shore to the godown. Thus this scene beautifully illustrates the power of positive believing.

When this bunch of villains comes to know that Amitabh was playing a double game with them and that he now intends on taking the same gold back to his boss, Iftekar, one of them says, *"Yaad rakho, yeh dushmani tumhe bahot mahengi padegi"* (This game will cost you very dearly). To which Amitabh very dramatically replies, *"Mein jab bhi kisse se dushmani karta hoon, saste aur mahenge ki parwa nahin karta"* (When I pick up a fight with someone, I don't bother about what it will cost me or what its repercussions will be).

Another story

Once upon a time there was a village that was facing a severe drought. It had not rained in this village for a long time. All the villagers were going through many hardships.

One day a sadhu baba came to the village and said, *"I will perform a pooja here tomorrow that will cause the rain to fall almost immediately".*

All the villagers were delighted as this baba's words were like the gospel truth to them and his words always came true.

The next morning, the entire village gathered at the spot chosen for the pooja. Only a small boy aged seven got an umbrella with him.

Why was this?

He was the only one to have a positive attitude and believed that the rain would actually fall and hence he came prepared with an umbrella.

Do you think the others really believed that the baba would make it rain or did they think he was just another fraud like Asaram Bapu?

Positive thinking is thinking that the desired event WILL happen tomorrow or in the future. Positive believing is believing that the desired event HAS ALREADY happened or is happening in the current tense.

Positive believing is about cheating ourselves into believing that the future is already the desired past or present (gift).

There's a thin line that separates positive believing from overconfidence. Always keep this in mind.

Chetan Bhagat, the bestselling author and one of the wittiest writers I have ever read, narrated an incident in one of his interviews that I must share with you.

During the university elections of his college, Chetan was confident (or overconfident) that he would win the elections. He went one step further. He was convinced that he would get all the votes and his opposition would get not more than one vote (his own vote). Being the kind-hearted guy he is, Chetan cast his own vote in the opposition's favor so that they would get at least two votes.

Chetan lost by one vote.

This is the way in which an overdose of positive believing can pose unthinkable challenges. So beware.

Positive believing is thinking that we have already received the things which we want; we have already achieved the outcome we desired.

This is not enough, you have to behave as if you have achieved everything.

If you want to be a CEO, behave like a CEO. If you want to get promoted to the next level in the corporate ladder, behave like the guy who is at the level at which you want to see yourself.

You should feel the way you would feel once you have achieved success. It is very important to be associated with those feelings as merely, believing and not feeling them may not give you the same results.

In the movie "Hera Pheri" by Priyadarshan which became a phenomenal success owing to the brilliant script adapted by the writer Neeraj Vora and executed with style by the actor Paresh Rawal, has one scene which describes positive believing.

Paresh already believes/ feels that he has received the money, which he is actually supposed to get the next day. With that conviction, he calls all his debtors and one by one tells them that he will be clearing their dues tomorrow. He even jokingly threatens them to come the next day or says, "I will come to your place to give the money".

He tells Peter, the alcohol supplier to fill the overhead tank with booze so that he can just open the tap and drink. This is positive believing at its best.

Positive believing is basically invoking the power of God.

God resides in everybody's hearts more than in temples, masjids or churches. People keep on searching for God their whole lives but God already resides in their hearts. Their search is as futile as that of a fish searching for water.

The God residing in our hearts is what I regard to be our subconscious mind. If only people would accept this surprising truth, we would have been able to get anything we wanted to from God, by listening to our own thoughts.

When our subconscious mind believes something to be true, it becomes true. Hence the power to achieve anything or the power to become anything we want, resides in us but we search for that power in the world outside.

A very long time ago, someone must have understood this miraculous fact of achieving anything you want by invoking the subconscious mind. But it is much harder to believe in your own self than to believe in someone else. This is the sad truth of our life. So in order to counter this, that man must have got a stone and told someone to keep this stone at his home and that by doing this he would get everything he wants in life. Now when the stone was installed, the person was able to believe that he could really get anything he wanted to. Hence his subconscious mind began to believe it too. Now since his subconscious mind believed it to be true, he achieved what he wanted to achieve and the credit went to that stone. He started worshipping that stone and believed in the power of that stone. That stone is the symbol of his subconscious mind. The same stone was given the name of God and we started worshipping it. Singing prayers and performing rituals are fine as they make us believe that we will achieve what we have set out to achieve. However we actually achieve whatever we achieve through our own mind. The belief that our actions will be successful is given by God. The concept of God was brought into this world by someone very smart. He wanted to make people invoke the power of their subconscious mind, though they were under the impression that they were invoking God. My belief is that God is nothing but a manifestation of our own subconscious mind.

Whatever you believe, you can achieve

I was attending a yoga class a few days ago and the instructor told us that while performing that particular asana, we had to believe that the asana was helping reduce all the toxic material in our body. Here also the importance of belief and believing comes across.

Believe and it is "God" or else it is just a stone. When you have complete belief or faith, that same God (or stone for some) will help you achieve everything you desire.

We are basically a mass of energy. When our hand is placed under a very advanced microscope, we see nothing but lots of entangled energy waves crisscrossing each other. These energy waves are waving or vibrating at a particular frequency. This frequency is determined by our thoughts. The way we think, the way our thought pattern operates, decides the various frequencies with which our energy waves oscillate. When we have positive thoughts in which we believe in our success, thoughts which assure us that the thing which we expect to get, is ours for the taking, we operate at a frequency which is exactly the same frequency at which the thing we want is operating at. Since these two frequencies are identical, they get attracted to each other. In other words, we attract what we want in life by operating at the frequency of belief, of having received. As a result we will indeed receive whatever we wanted to receive.

Now go get your dreams. They are yours for the taking!

◻◻◻

"Achieve new milestones and create records"

In the film "Lagaan", where Aamir Khan played the lead role, he was challenged by the Britisher to play the game of cricket. If the Indians won, the Britisher would not take any lagaan (tax) from them for next three years and if the Indians lost, the Britisher would take double the tax from them.

This seemed like an impossible task as until then, the Indians in the film were not even aware that such a game existed. Aamir Khan takes up the challenge; he wins the game and creates a record in the film. Even the film created a few records at the box office and went on to the Oscars.

From the gate of the Oscars to actually winning the ultimate trophy was also a big journey. In the telecom industry they call it "last mile connectivity". From succeeding in being nominated for the Oscars, the team's goal was to actually win a statuette. That was their main task. If that task was managed, Aamir and the rest of the Lagaan team could have laid their hands on the statuette and it would have now been in India.

Let me say something here about that fateful journey. Most of the time, it is not only talent but a lot of other factors which help you win or make you bite the dust.

In the corporate world, if somebody has to be promoted or apprised positively or negatively, it's not only his business numbers that speak but also his reputation or how he is perceived by others in the organization that matters a lot.

Once I was sitting with my colleague in his cabin. He was completing the appraisals of his team members, which were supposed to be sent that day itself, hence the rush. Suddenly we felt like having coffee and he called his office boy. The office boy walked in and to my utter horror (then it was horror, today I realize the mechanics behind that move), he asked the office boy, *"Naresh, what do you think of Rajesh Kumar?"* Meaning, did he get along with his team, colleagues, etc.? *"How does he treat you?"* Naresh was less than generous in his views about Rajesh. In fact, very subtly, he destroyed Rajesh's appraisal ratings. This means that because of Naresh's adverse feedback, he got his salary hiked by 10 % instead of 20 %, a sheer loss of a few precious lakhs. Why? Because someday somewhere because of right or wrong reasons he must have reprimanded Naresh and spoiled his relations with him. And now Naresh got back and hit him where it hurt the most. Yes, below the belt, but not where you were thinking. It is on his backside, where he keeps his purse. It became lighter for no visible mistake on Rajesh's part.

There is a lesson to be learnt here. In the corporate world, if you have to be tough or rude with someone so that the message gets to them and the same mistake doesn't get repeated, be tough or rude any way you choose but always remember to take that venom out of that man's mind after a few hours or a few days by some innocent gesture (from his point-of-view, though it may be a perfectly planned gesture from your side), which puts the aggrieved party in different mood. They may even start liking you again. Be extra friendly or anything but make sure the scars don't remain or else you have to pay by lakhs later on, due to those scars.

Records will only be created if we attempt to do something, which has not been achieved till then by anybody else.

Creating a "milestone" is the next target. There are many stones on the road but the stone at the end of the mile is called a "milestone" and is not called a mere stone. When you achieve something instead of sitting on your backside and soaking in the feeling of success (though you should celebrate and enjoy success for a couple of days as you deserve it), you should set the next target, the next "milestone".

In the corporate world, if you want to get ahead of the lot, you have to first see the record created in the past in your position and make plans to overcome that record. When you are swimming near the borders of the sea (not deep inside), the wave comes gushing at you, if you ride on the wave, you are pushed ahead but if the wave rides you, you are engulfed in it and pulled back, deep inside the sea, to die a watery death, maybe.

Similarly, in the corporate world, the wave (record) takes you forward.

Here, the wave should be created by you (checking the last highest performance) and you should ride it. Only this will provide you growth in all forms of life. Hence Reliance industry's tagline is *"Growth is life"*, very apt. In life, if we don't grow physically, we are as good as a dead vegetable. And if we don't grow intellectually, we are pulled backward.

In the movie "Deewar", goondas used to collect hafta (extortion money) from the hapless workers in the shipping dockyard. All the workers used to pay without uttering a word or asking why they have to hand over their hard earned money to line the goonda's pocket.

One day, a coolie refuses to pay and he is thrashed by the goons and 'accidently' gets run over by a speeding truck.

Next day, when all the coolies are sitting and chatting together during their usual break of a round of cutting chai, one old coolie says, *"Aaj tak hamne nahin dekha kissi coolie ko hafta na dete huen"* (Till today I have not seen anyone refusing to pay the hafta to these goons).

Amitabh says, *"Joh aaj tak nahin hua, woh ab hoga. Agle hafte, aur ek coolie in mawalionko hafta dene se inkar karne wala hai"* (What has not happened till today, will happen now. Next week, one more coolie is going to refuse to pay the extortion money to these goons).

Amitabh refuses to pay the next week and thrashes the goons and subsequently becomes the king of all goons in the movie. But the moral of the story is that Amitabh dared to achieve something which till then, nobody had ever thought of achieving.

In this movie, there is one more profound learning for all of us. Amitabh refuses to pay the hafta and hits the goondas asking for it. Then he goes to the canteen and sips a cup of chai. Down below the goondas have assembled with reinforcements (a few more goondas) and are frantically searching for Amitabh. They stop various coolies and ask them the whereabouts of Amitabh. They even stop the coolie who is always with Amitabh and Amitabh calls his Rahim chacha (uncle). By virtue of calling him "uncle", Amitabh also respects him like he would have respected his father's brother. The first learning is when you call someone with respect, please treat him with respect as well. When Rahim chacha comes to the canteen, he sees Amitabh, tells him in a worried tone that the goondas are searching for him downstairs. On hearing this Amitabh gets up and starts walking down as if he is confronting them face-to-face. On seeing this, Rahim chacha tells Amitabh to go the other way. The intention of Rahim chacha is simple. He does not want Amitabh to be found by these goons. Here Amitabh says, *"Sadak kya Peter (the head goonda) ke baap ki hai Rahim chacha?"* On hearing this, Rahim chacha gets agitated with worry for the safety of Amitabh and says, *"Dekh tu mujhe chacha kehta hai na? Toh yahan se mat ja, wahan se ja"*. Amitabh obediently listens to him (out of respect for elders) and goes out from the way shown by chacha. Here Amitabh gets a dua (blessing) from Rahim. That dua finally makes him victorious in the ensuing bloody fight with Peter's goondas. Today people depend on their talent and walk all over the people who have only good wishes for them like their parents, grandparents, friends, etc. The ultimate winner is the one who has "dua" on his side. Always remember that duas do more wonders then davas (medicines).

Sachin Tendulkar in one of his interviews, once said, *"There may be many more Sachins in the by lanes of Mumbai, who may be more capable and talented than me but I am what I am mainly because of all the blessings I have received"*. After being in the public glare for more than 25 years, show me one interview (written or on a television channel), where Sachin has bad mouthed anyone. I don't trust the views of so-called cricket experts (who may have faced lesser balls than what Sachin has hit in the nets). That said, in one of the interviews given by Ravi Shashtri (I have high regard for this sharp cricketing brain) he said or admitted honestly that, *"I have seen more cricket than what I have played and hence that itself gives me some authority to talk on the subject of cricket"*.

Getting back to the important confrontation between Amitabh and "Peter", the goon in Deewar. Subsequestly Amitabh goes from a different exit but straight away goes to Peter's den and waits for him there.

Peter's goons: *"Boss,woh kahin nahi mila. Lagta ha saala bhag gaya"*.

Peter: *"Bhagke jayega kahan? Aaj nahi toh kal hath mein jarror ayega. Usse zinda nahin chodne ka."*

At this very moment, Amitabh who is watching all this, sitting on a chair behind, calls out to Peter and says, *"Peter, tum log mujhe wahan dhoond rahe ho aur mein tumahara yahan intejar kar raha hoon"*. This act of Amitabh's displays courage. Instead of running away from problem, he is running towards the problem. As Ratan Tata had once said, *"Running away from the problem is the race one never wins"*. It is easier said than done. But here Amitabh does exactly what Ratan Tata was going to say 20 years down the line.

Amitabh locks that place where all these goondas are, i.e. the godown and throws the key to Peter and says, *"Isse apni jeb mein rakhna Peter. Ab mein yeh tala tere jeb se chaabi nikal kar hi kholunga"*. He is asking Peter to keep the key in his pocket and also challenges him that "I will open this door and that too, I will take the key out of your pocket and open the door". That calls for some real "balls of steel". Hats off to this courage and more than that, self-belief. It is more of self-belief that makes him victorious as Amitabh seemed to be well aware that he would hit all these goons black & blue and walk away from this godown with his head held high.

Thought gets converted into things. Spoken words become reality and in exactly the same way, thoughts gets converted into things. Bachchan hits them all and they are lying down. Suddenly Peter gets up wobbling and runs towards the door and tries to open it with his trembling hands. Bachchan comes running from behind doing some acrobatic stuff and hits Peter who falls down and apologetically tries to hand over the key to Bachchan. Now the learning. Bachchan asks him to put the key back in his pocket and says, *"Chabi jeb mein rakh Peter. Yeh tala mein tere jeb se chabi nikal ke hi kholunga"*. Bacchaan makes him put the key back in his pocket. He takes the key out himself and opens the door himself.

This is what it means to honour a commitment. Whatever commitment Bachhan gives to the goons, he manages to fulfil even that. Hats off to his integrity.

His actions were based on a promise he seemed to have silently made to himself that he will take the key from Peter's pocket and open the door himself.

Most of the guys I have seen in the corporate world, are content in knowing what the record is and are happy to reach for a target nearby. Then they will talk about how things were different for the guys who came before who achieved it and how things are difficult now, converting them into excuses, which justifies their disinterest to make an attempt at breaking the record.

Excuses and success can never travel together. They are like ice and fire. They are like Sharukh and Salman Khan. Though these two handsome gentlemen meet at an Iftar party thrown by a well-known politician every year, the unease they express at being in each other's company is clearly seen even in the photographs which eventually get splashed in the newspapers the next day.

Nobody knows what happened between them; two very good human beings who basically even after all these years are children at heart. Both live and die for others. Both live life king size.

I met one very successful music director. He is part of a group of musicians who give hit music to many of the current crop of films. While talking to him, he said there was a party where all the three big khans were present—Sharukh, Salman and Aamir. Some argument started between SRK and Salman Salim Khan (SSK), which soon turned ugly. During that altercation, SSK said something very nasty to SRK which hurt SRK no end. SRK being a true Scorpio, could never forget that humiliation. Hence whatever happens now doesn't matter to him, like Salman in interviews saying, "I like SRK. Maybe he is right in his dealings with others. I can't (even though I want to) deal with people like that and hence they take undue advantage of me. I don't allow anyone to badmouth SRK in front of me", etc., etc. Scorpions can forgive but never forget.

Something which happened between Arundhati Roy and SRK years ago still rankles SRK and he refuses to even acknowledge her. A Scorpion trait. SRK had once said in his interview *"If you walk on my toes, I will walk right into your face"*. It is a great statement for one to be able to succeed in today's world in general and corporate world, in particular. I have used this philosophy to my advantage many times in my professional dealings and got good result most of the times.

Salman may repent for what he said but his ego may be stopping him from going to SRK and hugging him (genuinely, not only for photo-ops) and saying sorry. These two guys had fought even earlier when they met at Farah Khan's wedding. They hugged each other, cried and cleared all cobwebs of distrust and anger. Let the history repeat itself and let all be well that ends well. SSK has an ego. EGO is Edging God Out. When you have ego, you put God out of you and then all your actions can only pull you down.

Sorry to digress but we were on the subject of success and excuses being at war with each other. I took a detour as I am more interested in the lives of film stars than I am in my own life. Subsequently, I even know more about their lives than they know themselves. Courtesy film magazines like Filmfare, Stardust, etc., also the TV show gossip about these stars, help me satiate my thirst for the tidbits about the lives these "guys and dolls" lead.

In the famous gazal in Umrao Jaan, the wording of one of the songs goes like this, *"Kahiye toh aasmaan ko zamee par utar laye, mushkil nahin hai kucch bhi agar than lijiye"* (You can even get the entire galaxy here on earth, nothing is impossible if you are determined to do it).

Impossible stands for *"I M Possible"*.

There are two types in the world. Successful individuals and individuals who are Failures. And as Sharukh says in "Happy New Year", *"Zindagi har failure ko moka deti hai, winner banneka"*. The universe gives one chance to all losers to become winners. One needs to grab that chance with both hands and even with both legs and turn himself into a winner. The reward of failure is oblivion.

The guys who want to create a new record and put their all in the pursuit of the same, are successful and the others who just want to get by, are survivors, at best and are otherwise branded failures.

These failures are lost even before the battle began as their mind has decided not to even try to come near that record, forget about overhauling it.

Try to excel not survive.

Sachin Tendulkar creates records not merely breaks them. Breaking somebody's record is good but then going so far ahead that all others cannot even dream of reaching there is creating a new milestone. Though someday someone with grit and determination can still trample that record to put his own stamp of excellence on it.

The best way to create the new record is not to bother yourself with the record/ result but to put all your energy in the work at hand, smartly and sharply.

When all your energies are directed towards the accomplishment of the set goal, you are working smartly. Wasting time/ energy in useless things on the way to the goal is working foolishly. In the Mahabharata Arjuna saw only the eye of the bird and nothing else when he was asked by his teacher to aim at the bird whereas all his brothers (both the pandavas and kauravas) saw the tree, the branches, the body of the bird, so on and so forth. Dushasan was even wondering whether the bird is a female or male. When you have your eyes on the goal, the goal is yours.

This reminds me of an Urdu couplet that goes thus, *"Hamari nazar to manzil pe hai, meel ke pathar hamne nahi dekhe"* (Our eyes were on the destination, we have not seen the milestones along the way).

When faced with grave challenges, some people break records, some people break down.

Records were created when you are up against seemingly impossible challenges.

If you are given a difficult/ very difficult/ near impossible task, you mentally accept defeat and move on. But if Yamraj (the merchant of death) gives you a near impossible task and says he will separate your body and soul (means he will kill you) if you don't achieve the task, the chances of you achieving the task successfully are 100%. Here again the mind cannot move on without successfully completing the task as it runs the risk of separating from the body i.e. it runs the risk of death.

Rockets move faster than aeroplanes. Why is this? Because there is fire under a rocket's backside.

Most of the times in a jungle, the prey though weaker than the predator, defeats the predator because while the latter is running for food, the prey is running for its life.

This desperate lunge towards the goal is one of the major reasons why people achieve their milestones or create records.

Graham Bell invented the telephone out of his frustration. His wife was partially deaf and he had to shout every time he had to communicate anything to her except saying *"I love you"* as that can be said through the eyes as well. He also symbolically said *"I love you"* to her by way of inventing the telephone so that he could communicate with her and at the same time, the whole world is grateful to the couple for making the entire universe communicate with each other seamlessly. By the way, the name of his wife was "Halo".

If you create records, you can go beyond death as even if you are no more, your records will keep you alive in everyone's hearts for longer duration.

Jai Ho!

❏❏❏

5

"First Impressions: Appearance and Body Language"

Making a good first impression depends on a number of factors, not just on your appearance.

When you appear for a meeting at the appointed hour, you have already set the stage for a positive interaction with your client. You appear 'once' in the sense that you need to appear only once for you to be able to make a favorable impression. You don't get a second chance to make your first impression. However, this matters only on your first visit; subsequent visits don't fall within this category. You have to, of course appear on time but along with this, you need to possess certain other tools. Without these 'tools', your client will see through you or worse still, judge you unfavorably, below your actual ability. What are these tools? We will explore this in further detail in this chapter.

Today people go by what their eyes see. If it is soothing to their eyes, they accept it. If not, they make a judgement. It is said that the eyes are the window to your soul. While this is true, judging by what I said earlier, it would appear that the person looking in through the 'window' is very superficial.

However, I think that what this statement is actually trying to say is that someone can actually reach your soul by looking into your eyes. If a man intently looks into the eyes of a woman and she meets his gaze with equal intensity they have an entire conversation without a single word being said. One falls in love with someone when one's soul starts loving the other soul. People who fall in love based on physical appearances can never understand the love of two people who see their partner's soul.

It is said that *Joh dikhta hai, woh bikta hai* (the thing which is seen, is sold). However such a transaction is very superficial and does not result in a long-lasting client relationship.

Appearances are not sufficient indicators of the quality of something. Take marriage for instance. There are many instances of two people falling madly in love with each other only to discover after marriage that they are constantly angry with their spouse. Physical attraction vanishes at the first instance of marital discord but soulful love can never reduce in intensity, no matter what physical challenges the partners face.

The movie "Queen" is a perfect example of the danger of judging a person only on their appearance. When Kangana Ranaut's charater is jilted at the mandap by her fiancé because he does not think she is modern enough to live with him in Europe, she proves him wrong by going on to travel across Europe on her own and make many friends along the way. In the end, her fiancé is the one who is shown to be small-minded and not as modern as she is.

I have a friend who was travelling by train many years ago when an accident happened. A 20-year-old girl had fallen off the train. People gathered around her and took her to a nearby hospital. She was treated there. Unfortunately one of her legs was amputated from below her knee. My friend often visited her in hospital as a courtesy and he fell in love with her. Was his attraction purely physical? Yes he liked the way she looked but his love was more about the meeting of two beautiful souls. This incident took place around 25 years ago and even today they are happily married.

So how do these examples translate into lessons for the world of business?

While it is important to dress well to make a good impression, it takes a lot more to build a strong relationship with your client. Does making a good impression mean wearing only branded products? Does the brand of your shirt, your pant, your shoes or belt, really matter? Most importantly, does the price of your mobile handset matter?

In the world we live in today, a lot of emphasis is placed on such considerations. This only means that the brands you choose have successfully managed to sell their idea to you— their product represents status. Take mobile phones for instance; today they are used for many purposes apart from merely talking. They are used to send letters and get your reply instantly; to send pictures, videos and audio messages; as a torch, calculator and camera; and as a digital diary. The day is not far when humanity will succeed in transporting a person from point A to point B through their mobile phone. Don't raise your eyebrows at such a far-fetched idea. No doubt there were people who raised their eyebrows when Wright brothers said they would make metal fly, along with people.

Today, the biggest and most important use of a mobile phone is that to most people, it seems to convey a lot about your bank balance. A mobile phone is expensive, and thus owning one implies that you have a big bank balance. This, to some people, implies that you seem to be earning quite well in your chosen profession. People want to deal with successful people and thus such people, to whom owning an expensive phone is a symbol of their status in society, will get drawn into doing business with you. Of course a mobile phone is not a real indicator of your success in your profession such as your ability to take care of your financial responsibilities towards your parents and family. However, in the world of business, it is important.

Now just owning an expensive phone is not enough, you must also learn to carry it with style. For example if you handle your cellphone with a lot of care—keeping it in a nice pouch, talking on it and carefully replacing it in its pouch, handling it as if it was your first lady love—your client will realise that you can ill afford such an expensive handset. He may think that either you have bought a stolen product from the chor bazaar in Mumbai or that you have bought a second-hand piece or that it is a gift from Bajaj/ Tata, that is, bought using a loan from Bajaj or Tata finance. You should handle the handset the way you handle a wife who is married to a man for two decades—casually and informally. I have seen immensely wealthy men sitting at a hotel table with me, casually throwing their phone in one corner of the table. Such an attitude is that of a man accustomed to luxury and gives people the idea that he is prosperous and successful.

Moving on, I think it is important to state that the best things in life cannot be bought and are priceless, such as the smile of a six-month-old child and a good night's sleep. You can give birth to a child but its smile cannot be bought. You can buy the most expensive bed but you can't buy sleep. You can marry a woman but can't buy her love. One can buy a body but not its feelings.

The list of "best things in life," includes a few more important things. A man/ woman can wear a million dollar dress but he/ she looks attractive only when he/ she wears a smile. As is well known—a smile is the shortest distance between two individuals; a smile is a curve on your face but it straightens lots of complex issues of your life. There's a reason why Madhuri Dixit's smile is so famous. Unlike other actors, her smile appears to radiate from her own inner happiness, which is why it does something to her audience.

A smile is infectious. Our brain has mirror neurons which reflect whatever comes in front of our eyes. When you smile (are a happy person), the mirror neurons in a person looking at you reflect your happiness and they feel happy. Similarly when a client sees your smile, his mirror neurons give him a shot of happiness, he becomes happy and he is inclined to do business with you because somewhere deep inside, your smile has smoothened a few frayed nerves.

Dhamakedar first look: How to select the right dresses and accessories

Appearance leads to clearance. These two words, spelt similarly are closely related in the dictionary of a good sales person. If you need clearance from a customer (for your proposal) in two seconds, your appearance makes all the difference. It has to be top class.

Crumpled, faded or torn shirts, faded shoes and watch straps, half-grown beards, oiled hair, ink-stained fingers, canvas bags, extremely colourful clothes, etc., all result in people making snap judgements about you. It is important to take care of every detail of your appearance from your hair and nails to the pen in your pocket and the watch on your wrist. It is a good practice to always be well-groomed and neat as it shows that you have your life in control and that you have time to take care of small details.

As a next step, you can consider investing in a few branded products to make your wardrobe stand out. Have you heard about brands such as Mont Blanc, Louis Philippe, Allen Solly, Ray-Ban, Woodlands, Arrow, etc.? These are just the names of a few; there are thousands of such brands in the market. It doesn't hurt to do some window-seeing to know more about the brands that you can afford and add to your wardrobe. Every big brand has an "end of season" sale that makes their products all the more affordable so watch out for those. Wearing a good quality branded product really helps in making a favorable first impression.

It's no secret that the world, especially the world of sales, is dominated by the use of expensive material things. So what comes first? Expensive material things or the right attitude to your business? The chicken or the egg?

You may be pardoned if you don't want to take too many risks and are content making a few good bucks by being in the business of sales and waiting for a chance, after earning a good sum of money, to go for those expensive things such as a

Louis Philippe shirt, Allen Solly pant, Rolex or Titan (at least) watch, Woodland shoes, Ray-Ban sunglasses, the latest model of Apple iPhone, etc.

But such a careful approach to sales could result in failure. Any business needs investment and the business of sales, 'needs' the investment of accessories. The fall-out of making such investments is that you may have to beg, borrow or steal the required sum to purchase what you need. It is for this reason that it makes sense to find a balance between owning a few expensive things and maintaining a degree of smartness in everything else that you own and most importantly, wearing a smart attitude like Ranbir Kapoor in "Rocket Singh: Salesman of the Year".

There is a saying in Hindi, which goes as follows: Mahenga kharide to pachtaye ek baar, saasta kharide to pachtaye baar baar. Simply translated this means if you buy something expensive you repent once but if you buy something cheap you repent repeatedly as it will keep bothering you with its problems (it will also bother you in another way; it will result in you being neglected by the very people you want to impress).

Buying nice things for yourself is beneficial in another way. If you are feeling good about yourself, others will also feel good about you. One of the ways of feeling good about yourself is to dress well, dress clean and sometimes, dress expensive.

The other way you can feel good about yourself is by doing something for somebody with no expectation of anything in return. If you feed a street kid a packet of biscuits or a few chocolates, the swell in your heart will be so aggressive that you will be able to take on your toughest adversary even in torn clothes. In the film "The Pursuit of happyness", Will Smith's character goes for an interview in shabby clothes but still his inner confidence and wittiness is such that it gets him the job. This is not to advocate shabby clothing but if you are not able to purchase expensive add-ons, don't lose heart, you can still win but you need to be very resourceful and have tremendous courage (balls of steel).

The bottom line is this, one has to give lots of attention to the way one presents oneself to the world. However, apart from your physical appearance there are a few other things which contribute to how the world perceives you.

Chakachak smile: Letting your inner happiness shine

One accessory which is completely free but used by very few people is a smile.

As the world knows, a smile can bridge the distance between two strangers. In foreign countries, people greet each other in lifts, parking lots and malls with a smile. In India, a husband waits for a naughty smile from his wife and vice versa but the wait never ends. A subordinate employee waits for an appreciative smile from his boss and in India, the boss never expects his subordinate to smile or else he feels, he is not a good manager. In India, if your subordinate is terrified of you, you are a great manager. This notion, while being ridiculous, is the truth. In India, most of the time, managing people is perceived to be the same as controlling them through brute force or though black mail. This is not what I believe. A smile does not result in a loss of control or a loss of respect from the people who work for you. A smile builds trust and it is only when people trust you that they follow your leadership.

When people fear you or feel manipulated, they try their best to subvert your authority, which eventually leads to failure. Besides as a leader, you must always make an example of your behaviour, that is, behave the way you want your subordinates to behave. Shah Rukh Khan in "Chak De! India" is accepted by the women of the Indian hockey team who follow his tough orders during practice and on the field only because he shows them that he respects them as athletes and doesn't dismiss their abilities because they are women. He shows them that he trusts them. Although he doesn't smile much in the movie, when he does, it changes his personality completely.

Thus a smile can add a lot of weight to your overall appearance. An average-looking face lit by a smile comes across as far more endearing than a good-looking, grumpy face.

When you have a smile on your lips, your face conveys the inner happiness you feel about yourself, your surroundings and the overall turn of events in your life. If a lot of good things are happening in your life, a smile always remains on your face. If a lot of unpleasant, unwanted things are happening in your life, your face looks grumpy.

A smile on your face conveys not only that you are happy but it also conveys that you are successful personally, professionally, physically, spiritually, etc. It is natural for everyone to want to be associated with a successful guy and people will be drawn towards you if you wear a radiant smile. This isn't to say that you must paste a fake smile on your face even if you are dealing with serious personal problems. Fake smiles do not produce the same kind of effect. For a smile to be effective it is important to believe that you are happy. When people say that happiness is a state of mind, what do they mean? They mean that being happy is independent of external circumstances. You either believe you are happy or you don't. In the world today, there is always going to be something that makes you feel like a failure, makes you feel defeated. If it's not a colleague making you feel like he is more important than you, it's your parents comparing you with your siblings, or life itself dealing you a cruel blow through the death of a loved one. At moments like these, you must always remember to list all the things that make you a success and a good human being. Count all the ways in which you are a good person, and you have made a difference to someone else's life. In this way you will find that you are happy almost all the time.

Happiness produces certain behavioral patterns and so does sadness. We are so much in sync with these patterns that we subconsciously follow them when we feel happy or sad.

Our subconscious mind consists of impressions that are made when we are conscious. Thus if you consciously laugh out loud as though you have been showered by a torrent of happiness even when you are in an excruciatingly sad situation, your subconscious mind will feel that you are happy and it will reciprocate with happy feelings and most importantly, it will aid in creating happy situations in your life.

If you find laughter therapy difficult, don't hesitate to take a pause from your busy schedule to do something that cheers you up. Visit a friend, take beautiful photographs, spend time with your pets, take a walk down a road with tall trees, and feed the birds that come to your window, cook something exotic. Do things that open your soul to the world around you and your problems will fade into the background. When this happens your smile will return to your face before you know it.

Dhating Nach: Showing enthusiasm in everything you do

The next important thing that makes a good impression is enthusiasm. Nothing in the world has been achieved without enthusiasm. Enthusiasm draws things to you and a lack of enthusiasm repels them, even if you deserve them.

A man with less talent but a lot of enthusiasm can win even if he competes with a talented but laid-back super human.

As discussed earlier, people who perceive you as being successful will start to like you and this will allow you to get what you want from them. So coming across as successful is important. Enthusiasm portrays you as successful. How is this?

When a man is on a mission to accomplish something and he can envision this achievement in his mind's eye, he becomes desperate, in his actions, words, etc., to reach his goal. I view this desperate urge to reach a goal as enthusiasm. So in a way, an enthusiastic man sees himself as already in possession of what he is trying to achieve. This means his body behaves as if it is already in possession of that success and hence his enthusiasm is taken as a sign of success already achieved. Enthusiasm can also be seen as a spirit to never give up and to keep fighting for what you believe in. Farhan Akhtar as Milka Singh shows exactly such killer instinct when he aims for an Olympic gold medal in "Bhaag Milkha Bhaag".

If you perceive your target to be far-fetched and difficult, if not impossible to achieve; if you are not ready to pay the price for your goal, your body language conveys your unhappiness and you react to everything very slowly and in a dis-interested manner. This can be interpreted by the people who meet you as a lack of desire to achieve your goal. This may result in someone else being awarded a contract that could have been yours.

Negativity is difficult to hide. Thus a person who believes he will fail, is also responsible for his failure. When you don't have faith in yourself it is difficult for others to have faith in you, and as a result, you fail to impress them.

Mein Hoon Superman: Displaying quiet confidence

An empty truck, when passing by, makes a lot of noise, but when the same truck is loaded, it travels silently without making any noise. Similarly, a man with a lot of substance carries himself quietly without making any tall claims, fuss, etc., as he is quite sure of himself and his abilities; like Superman, who works as an anonymous news reporter who no one gives credit to for all his achievements but who saves the world anyway. Such a realization, that the acceptance of others is secondary to one's own achievements is *"quiet confidence"*.

It is better that other people blow your trumpet as nobody is interested if you brag about your own achievements. Likewise a man who is not boasting much but whose work is exemplary, comes across as a person who can do a lot without saying a lot.

Confidence is the sign of a person who believes that he is going to achieve what he sets out to achieve. Again as mentioned earlier, people get attracted to success and this confident guy/ gal is success personified. Hence he/ she is instantly liked by all and sundry.

Nawabi Tehzeeb: Having the manners of a king

Manners are un-enforced standards of conduct which demonstrate that the person is proper, polite and refined. Two words which more or less define you as a well-mannered guy are *"Please"* and *"Thank you"*. Few other words to add to your list of manners are "Excuse me" and "I am sorry". Knowing when to use these words so that they have maximum impact also is the mark of a well-mannered individual. Bosses often order their subordinates to do things, but their stock will rise by many miles if they ask using the prefix of *"Please"*. When they show respect, more often than not, they will find their work completed by their subordinates without a lot of follow-up. By saying *"Thank you"* after the job is done, they will ensure that the next time the job will be completed without them having to ask about it. That is the power of these innocuous sounding words.

However, most importantly, manners reveal that you are a man/ woman of integrity. They reveal that you are not trying to manipulate your client, cheat them or lie to them. You are treating them with respect and you truly believe what you are selling. They also reveal how observant and sensitive you are. When you notice the discomfort of another person and act in such a way that you alleviate it, then they will view you differently. How does one become more observant? The answer to this is fairly simple; by opening yourself to new experiences and by trying to understand the world through the eyes of another person (by showing empathy). Many forms of literature and art, help you expand your understanding of other human beings. Therefore the more you read, the more refined and observant you become.

Akshay Kumar in one of his movies says *"Agar tum aurat ko izzat doge, woh apni izzat tumhe degi"*. Which translates to—If you respect a woman, she will offer her respect (in this dialogue, her respect is equated with her body) to you. Even though this dialogue was written to evoke a few laughs, it carries behind it a serious philosophy.

If you respect someone sincerely, in return he will respect you. He will genuinely feel like respecting and helping you. He will want to be in your company and given the opportunity, will help you somehow. In short, he will be drawn towards you.

Manners don't cost you a paisa but reward you a lot. And you don't have to be wealthy to have good manners.

Amitabh Bachchan never stays seated if he spots a woman around him who is standing. That is a result of his upbringing and his manners. Dilip Kumar says about Amitabh *"He is a man of fine breeding"*.

Finally, we must note that good manners are infectious. You will find that the children of well-mannered parents also turning out to be well-mannered and the reverse, sadly, is also true.

❑❑❑

"Knowing your Customer: Separating the Potentials from the Bloodsuckers"

When does a customer finally agree to an appointment? It could be because of one of the following reasons:

1. Your follow-up was very strong. You kept calling no matter what excuse he gave you, postponing your conversation to a later date. After a point, he started feeling guilty and hence agreed to meet you for a few minutes, giving you a chance to sell your wares.

2. He got interested in the brief value proposal (consisting of an attractive cost benefit analysis; customer gets the value while he pays the price) you recommended to him on the phone and now he has agreed to allow you to cross confirm your telephonic words with a face-to-face meeting.

3. He just gave you an appointment because he could not say "No". Most of humanity lies within this dreadful category. For some, it is easy to say "Yes" but virtually impossible to say "No". As Amitabh Bachchan says in the movie Agneepath, *"Zindagi mein aage badhne ke liye, Na bolna bahut zarrori hai"* (It is very important to say "No", if you want to

move ahead in life).

4. He wants you (the salesperson) to come and give him free gyan (knowledge) and then get lost. These people are forever looking out to gain something for nothing in exchange. There is yet another category even worse than this one, which I will explain with an example:

There was a man who always looked for an opportunity to get something for nothing or next to nothing. One day, he went to purchase a shirt in a shopping mall. He visited many shops, checked on the style and price of several shirts and finally zeroed in on one shirt which matched what he had in mind. But there was a catch; though the shirt matched his liking, it woefully fell short with respect to his expectation of its price. He started to bargain. The salesperson was smart. He had to liquidate all his stock in the next one month as the shop was shifting to a new premises and did not want to take any old stock with them so he had nothing to lose by playing along with the customer. Thus the negotiations began. The customer first suggested a ridiculous price. After some hesitation the salesperson accepted it. The customer got confused. He suddenly felt that he probably should have bargained some more, so he asks for an even lower price. To his amazement, the sales guy accepted this new lowered price as well. Now the customer was completely perplexed. He continued to bargains pushing the sales guy to lower the rate even further. This went on and on until, finally, the customer asked the sales guy to give him the shirt, believe it or not, for free! The sales guy, hell bent on getting this inventory out of his shop door, agrees. Now the customer is elated but still not satisfied. So what does he do now? He suggests that since the salesperson is giving him the shirt free of cost, he give him two shirts instead of one. Now the sales guy loses patience and what he said to the customer is unprintable. Let's come to the main point. Such customers are real parasites as they don't give a damn about the sales guy's feelings and are only interested in their own feelings, almost always. That day is not far for people in this category, when the whole world, including their near and dear ones, will stop having any feelings for them.

5. He wants to see whether he can use you or your contacts for some of his other work. These guys are similar to the ones in the previous category, but at least they have some idea about what they will/ should get from you, unlike category four, who will do anything to get something for free. This reminds me of a story. A small fish asked her mother, *"Who are these people who walk on roads? Why are they not in the water like us?"* The mother said, *"We are fish and they are selfish"*. True black humour indeed.

Before you reach the office door of your customer, you should say, *"I am the best. I am a champion,"* to yourself at least 20 times with your eyes closed, keeping your mind blank. Believing in these utterances will help you better your confidence levels and thus make you better at what you do. The great boxer Mohammed Ali, used to repeat these two lines for at least 30 minutes before his boxing matches. Believing it, while saying it, will work wonders. Feel the way the boxing champion did. Hold your chin up and your head high. Believe that you are God's greatest gift to humankind and that you are born to win this business deal, which will help the customer more than YOU!

The important point that I'm trying to make here is, for you to understand and recognise that the buyer is going to benefit more than the seller. When you feel this, your body language communicates this to the customer even without your knowledge. And unfortunately, this plan can also backfire on you if you aren't too careful and seem overconfident. Your body language is also capable of saying, *"Hey customer, you are the biggest mamu (Meaning uncle. Please refer to Munna bhai MBBS). I will be benefitting from this deal tremendously but I'm not sure how you will benefit from it."*

Believe me, the most potent communication is conducted always, I repeat, always without words.

I remember Anil Kapoor stating in one of the interviews, that during his early years of struggle, he met the famous Telugu film director Sattiraju Lakshminarayana, known by his nickname "Bapu". After a lot of pestering by Anil, Bapu agreed to include him in one of his movies. The only problem was that movie was in Tamil. Bapu asked Anil about his proficiency in Tamil. Anil, in a moment of overflowing enthusiasm, told Bapu that he knew Tamil very well and could speak his lines with ease. Bapu said Ok and asked him to report on the sets in a few days. Now Anil was worried. He had got a role in an alien language and did not know what to do. He then went to the person whom he considered to be the best actor India has ever produced, the great Naseeruddin Shah. On listening to Anil's problem, Shah told Anil that he did not need to talk to show his feelings. He asked him to understand the scene and act; everything else including language would fall in place. This example underlines my argument that the significance of words does not compare to that of body language either in movies or in a business scenario.

Have you spent time visiting a children's park with your son or daughter? Have you noticed how when two children are playing together, they communicate with each other perfectly without using too many words. In fact, sometimes words fail to justify the true feelings which you are experiencing. Hence the saying, I am happy beyond words.

Consider this scenario: You walk into the office and begin talking to the receptionist, Pinky. You tell her that you have an appointment with Mr Saxena at 11 am.

The cardinal rule here is that the clock should strike 10:45 am, when you have this golden conversation with the empty-headed beauty (which I have found to be a general trend in most offices but this is not always true as I have also had the opportunity to meet a few killer beauties with menacingly sharp and alert grey cells) behind the reception desk.

When you talk to the receptionist, it is very important to note that you should be seen as totally disinterested in her (your eyes should not reveal that you are immensely attracted to her because this is what she expects from you or this is what she expects your eyes to betray).

Now your disinterest in her, will force her to give you importance and you should behave as if YOU ARE God's gift to women (mentally play the "Set Wet" deodorant advertisement in your uncontrollable mind) and thus you succeed in cultivating a mole, an informant, in the best possible position in the office.

Now you are waiting to be called inside. The time is around 10:48 am. You have at least 12 minutes to go inside. Ask Pinky about the whereabouts of the washroom. After she tells you where the washroom is, don't thank her just say Ok. In today's big bad corporate space, courtesy is treated as a weakness. First we need to establish our strength in any situation and after it is established, I repeat only after it is established, your courtesy will be treated as courtesy and not as a weak-kneed gesture. On the way and back from the washroom, your eyes and ears should be open for any potential information which will help you close the sale. You can strike a brief conversation with somebody who is inside the loo. You have to talk to the office boy who will give you glass of water when you go to pantry. Now you can get some data here which will be very important for closing the sale in your favour and going to the bank, all the way, laughing.

You should also consider asking Pinky a few superficially harmless, innocent questions. Remember, you are trying to get some information which will help you close the sale faster. Don't stray while talking to her as that can be a huge trap as you could lose the focus on the business objective of the visit.

These few minutes should help you know the whereabouts of the POPAT.

I will explain what I mean by POPAT with the help of a story, which you may have heard from your nanny when you were a kid. I am sure, your nanny also must have heard this ancient fable from her nanny when your nanny was a just a kid and not a nanny.

Once upon a time, there was a monster who was beating all the people of a village and harassing everybody. People fired bullets at him, threw stones at him, planted RDX bombs in his undergarments but to no effect. He was invincible because he had kept his life (jaan /pran /spirit, whatever you wish to call it) in a parrot (please don't ask me which body part of the parrot it was hidden in). He had then hidden the parrot far away in an unknown place which nobody knew. All the attacks on this monster were useless. He was unmoved and unaffected by the villagers efforts to kill him because his parrot was safely hidden somewhere else. The location of this parrot was only known to the monster.

One day, one smart guy like the one who is reading this now, came to the village.

On hearing the predicament of the villagers, he decided to help them by getting rid of this dastardly monster. He wanted to find out the way to kill him as he was told that every effort to kill him had been futile. He met the monster and his cronies, he befriended them, made them talk about the monster and made the monster talk about himself.

After repeated seemingly harmless but probing questions, the smart guy comes to know about the whereabouts of the parrot. The smart guy goes to the parrot and kills him. He thus succeeds in killing the monster without even touching him. This is bloodless surgery or a bloodless murder.

All the while when you were at the washroom, pantry, reception, etc., you should only look out for the whereabouts of the parrot.

In a scene from Trishul, when Amitabh Bachchan meets Sanjiv Kumar for the first time, R K Gupta, played by Sanjiv Kumar says, *"Mere paas tumhare liye sirf paanch minute hai"*.

Here Vijay (the character played by Amitabh), doesn't exchange any pleasantries and directly gets to the topic as he values his and the opposite person's time and wants to end the meeting well within the five minutes allotted to him and at the same time he wants the meeting to be fruitful for both of them. Vijay says, *"Agar meri information galat nahi hai toh saath saal (seven years) pehle aapne ek zameen kharidi thi, theen lakh rupeh (three lakh rupees) mein. Aaj uski kimat kam-se-kam paanch lakh (five lakhs) hai, magar aapke yeh paanch lakh doobe huye hai, kyonki wahan kisi Madho Singh naam ke goonde ka kabja hai".* (If my information is correct, 5 years ago you had purchased one plot of land for Rs. 3 L. The current value of that land must be Rs. 5 L but you have currently lost that money because one bully (Madho Singh) has illegally captured that land.)

To which Gupta replies, *"Haan, yeh sab toh mein bhi janta hoon, magar yeh mere doobe huye paise tum mujhe kaise wapas dila sakte ho?"* (Yes, I am well aware of this information but how can you help me get this lost money back to me?)

Sales is nothing but getting the needs (hidden or expressed) of the customer to the surface and converting those needs into wants. Make sure your customer first acknowledges the problem he has, before jumping in with a solution.

Golden rule 1: Offer water to someone only when he is thirsty or else he may wash his bum with the mineral water you have given him.

Golden rule 2: Make him thirsty.

Golden rule no 3: Use rule No. 2, before you attempt rule No. 1.

Let us not be like politicians, who promise us bridges where there is no river.

Once your customer accepts the challenge he is facing, make him ask for the solution. A good salesperson does not sell, they only give customers what they ask for. The only difference between a good salesperson and a bad salesperson is, the good salesperson will play his cards in such a way that the customer himself will ask for his product. Let us not sell, let us make the customer buy and we should come across as someone who helped the customer buy the solution he needed so badly in the first place.

Once the customer asks for the solution, give it to him and ask him to pay the price for the solution immediately before he comes up with any objections.

This is very important as when the problem is accepted by customer, he asks for a solution. When the solution is given by the sales guy and he states his price (ask for a cheque), the customer begins to raise objections.

Now the key is to take a conditional commitment from the customer before you take care of his objections and explain the solution for each of the customer's objections.

The real sale starts after the objection is raised. To be able to solve the customer's objections, is what "sales" is all about. The interaction before the objection raises its head is at best called a presentation but can never be called sales, as that is not sales at all.

For example consider saying this, "If I solve all your queries to our mutual satisfaction, will I get the cheque today?" If he says YES, solve the objections and pick up the cheque. If he says, it will take a few days before I arrive at a purchase decision even after the objections are resolved, DON'T give any explanation to his objections.

As it is foolish to solve his objections today and come after one month to collect the cheque. I have found that 99 percent of the time, customers just raise some new objections during the interim period and the sale keeps getting postponed.

Hence the key is, provide your customers with solutions only when they are willing to give you a cheque immediately.

Mall culture is mushrooming. People love going inside the mall; touching and feeling the things they are thinking of purchasing. This makes them go into an emotional state (irrational, most of the times) resulting in instantaneous purchases that take place with just one bloody swipe (I will explain in later chapters, why this swipe is so bloody as you need to understand that it is your own blood, which is being shed).

Ask these people to come after 30 minutes to buy the same product. I am willing to bet that 99% of the time they will not buy it.

You can't do the foreplay, undress a woman and then tell her you want to go for a walk for 30 minutes. Do u think she will wait for you?

If you think so, you are not in your senses as she will purchase the required goods before she closes her shop (no pun intended please.)

Coming back to "Trishul", R K Gupta says, *"Haan, magar yeh mere doobe huye paisee, tum mujhe kaise wapas dila sakte ho?"* (How can you get me, my stuck money?) To which Vijay replies, *"Mein yeh zameen kharidna chahata hoon."* (I want to buy this land) RK Gupta objects to this. He says, *"Yeh jante huye bhi, ki mere wakil pichle cheh saal (6 years) se use wahan se nikalne ke liye nakamyab huye hain?"* (Even after knowing this that my lawyers have been unsuccessful for last 6 years in the pursuit of getting the land vacated?)

To which Vijay says, *"Haan. Yeh jante huye bhi mein ye zameen kharidna chahata hoon."* (Yes, I want to buy this land even after knowing this)

(RK Gupta expected Vijay to be taken aback. If he had done that he would have betrayed the confidence which he had in the product. Here the product is "Vijay" himself as "Vijay" has to get the land vacated.)

So when a customer throws objections at us, they are not objections about the product/ service per se, but he is testing your confidence in the product/ service.

For example, somewhere in 1999-2000, I was flying to Nagpur from Mumbai in an Alliance flight (Alliance air details can only be found in the pages of ancient history). The condition of the flight was no better than a 99-year-old woman trying to romp in bed.

En route, the flight was making a lot of weird noises. The guy sitting next to me was terrified as he thought we are not going to follow the ATC's (Air Traffic Controller's) instructions for landing and instead we will immediately go down vertically and then go up (to heaven / hell, depending on the number of females you have cheated in your life or the truckload of sins you have committed in life) vertically.

I was also scared but I was observing the air hostesses. You dirty mind, don't get me wrong. I was looking for signs of panic in them. If they had panicked, I would have also panicked, but they were cool (even though they looked hot) and hence I knew these noises were routine and that I will continue to live for a few more decades at least.

Coming back to the sales situation, the customer is observing panic reactions in you. If you don't display panic or on the contrary display confidence, the customer will buy your product (at the cost of repetition, I will say that actually he is buying your confidence in the product).

While the customer buys the product irrationally (From a buyer's point of view: you should not judge the quality or usage of the product through salesman's body language only), he justifies his buying decision to himself and the world rationally. Isn't this strange? But yes, the customer will find the sales points and USPs etc., of the product (even if you fail to do so) when he is justifying his purchase decision to himself, his wife or family.

Key learning: Believe in yourself, your company and the product. If the belief is sold, the product itself becomes immaterial.

Final golden rule: The customer buys three things necessarily in the same order, which are—Person, Organisation, Product/ service i.e. solution.

A customer does not buy your product/ service; he buys your confidence in the product/ service.

To sum it up, your first meeting with the customer should lead to business or in the worst case, the confirmed date of your next meeting.

If your first meeting goes bad, you go out of business, at least with this customer. If you don't learn fast, you will be out of everything, forever. But I am sure, you will surely scale new heights in your corporate/ business career, if you keep the pearls of wisdom mentioned in this chapter in mind whenever you try to make a sales pitch.

Happy first date with your customer!

❏❏❏

7

"Internal customer, external customer and growth"

When you work in an organization, you believe that your achievements on certain business parameters are what will take you to the next level. This is partly, and I reiterate, strictly only partly true. Your real growth comes through interactions with your colleagues. You find this strange? Let me explain…

When your appraisal is done by your superior and he is mulling over what ratings he should give you and suddenly the office boy enters his cabin with tea and your boss happens to ask him what he thinks of you, do you think what he says will make a difference to your rating? Believe it or not, the office boy's comments about you can make or break your career in that organization.

Your boss while smoking in the parking lot may again casually enquire about you to your colleagues and what they say has immense bearing on your prospects of upgradation or your degradation. Now please note that the office boy and your colleague will not talk about your achievements on specific business parameters; that is not their concern. They will talk good about you if you were good to them, period. Hence your equation with the internal customers of your organization, i.e. your peon, receptionist, colleagues, etc., will have a direct impact on your future.

The receptionist also holds a lot of keys to the secrets of the organization. Sometimes the boss's keys are also in her hands (no pun intended). Remember Gauhar Khan's role in the film Rocket Singh: Salesman of the Year? Without her help, Ranbir Kapoor's character would not have been able to achieve the success that he does. As a receptionist, she is undervalued in the organisation, but Singh sees her potential. She helps Singh identify promising prospective clients.

I have worked in a few Small and Medium-sized Enterprises (SMEs) after I passed out of engineering college. In the beginning, I joined a small company that used to import office copiers in India and sell them. Here the owner was the Boss. He was middle aged and had a very attractive but married secretary. I used to hear a lot of gossip about them but I never believed them because she was a great person, came across as a very decent woman and had a small five-year-old daughter. Even her husband used to visit our office and he used to get some work from our boss. Later however, I happened to be in a situation (the details of which I will not get into) in which all those rumours were confirmed. In fact on that day my value systems and beliefs were shaken to the core. Anyway, in this company, she was the de-facto boss. She used to take all or most of the decisions and the boss used to endorse her views. That she was very smart and sharp was probably one of the reasons why she was given so much authority but no doubt her efficiency in bed was the major reason for the power she wielded over my boss. She had him completely under her spell. Such a situation is not very shocking. Office escapades are a lot more commonplace than most people realize. Office sexcapades, affairs, etc., have been happening for a long time and will continue till the end of humanity. Why is this? The main reason, I believe is connected to the amount of time people spend at office. If you look closely, the working man or woman spends more time with his/ her male and female office colleagues than with his/ her own spouse.

Coming back to our point of discussion, which is the internal customer. If you are a great asset to the organization and are winning several lucrative business deals for your company but you fight with this secretary, you will not make any headway as far as your vertical growth in the organization is concerned. You have to be at your best and on your guard more inside the office than outside the office.

N. R. Narayana Murthy (NRN), the Founder of Infosys once said, *"My people are my real assets. Every evening they go out of my premises and it is my duty to see that they come the next day all charged up to over-deliver on their job responsibilities."* Infosys is doing well mainly because of this attitude. Currently they are under a cloud and not doing well (The new poster boy from SAP AG, Vishal Sikka, may succeed in changing the scenario) because in spite of having huge cash reserves, they are neither showing signs of growth (as they are playing it safe, which is one of the biggest reasons for the downfall of any big organization) nor hiking the salaries of their staff, who are their assets. An asset will appreciate in value only if you add value (in this case a monetary hike) to it.

One of the first things that Sikka did on accepting office was to hike employee remuneration. The salaries of top management increased by three to six times. Now, Infosys employees are paid on par with their overseas counterparts who are paid in dollars. This will help Sikka retain them from poachers. With their domain expertise (in the IT industry in general and Infosys in particular), it is only a matter of time before the company surges ahead.

Infosys demands a margin of 28% for their services, which are built on the backs of motivated employees (as in NRN era). It is foolish to expect the same margin with de-motivated employees. I sometimes wonder, why such a simple fact was not noticed by S D Shibulal, the former CEO of Infosys and the rest of the company's management and board. Committing financial fraud is not the only way to mismanage a company, taking foolish decisions and being negligent also fall under the category of mismanagement. If things don't improve at Infosys, this might as well be the beginning of the glorious end.

Vineet Nayar of HCL has written a book titled "Employees First, Customers Second:" Turning Conventional Management Upside Down. This is precisely the reason why HCL is doing far better than Infosys and will one day overtake Infosys.

Our employees are our link to customers. The boss is not actually managing customers, he is managing the people who manage customers, i.e. who manage the business. Hence the mismanagement of employees will result in the mismanagement or worse still, abuse and ill treatment of the end users or customers.

Companies who ignore this fact soon go into the past tense.

The legendary lack of motivation in government employees

Why are government employees not bothered about their work and completely demotivated?

This is the most well-guarded secret of the country, which every employee of a government department has been able to hide from the Government of India.

People who join any organization, join with certain aspirations. They want to achieve something, do something worthwhile for the organization. Nobody joins and says, now I will enjoy the rest of my professional life of 40 years by doing absolutely nothing. There may be exceptions to this rule but by and large people want to be productive and achieve something in their lives.

When a bright or dull young man joins, he wants to contribute and add value as per his mental and physical capabilities. In the government, when he tries to do something, he is faced with complete lethargy and indifference from existing staff who have been there for the last 25-30 years. He finally gets completely frustrated and just waits for the clock to strike six so he can go home. When this new employee strives to do something, the old man (Jo kabr mein pair latkake baitha hain) discourages him (which is an understatement). Without anybody's support and help, this new guy is not able to achieve anything and one-fine-day he throws up his hands and joins the ranks of those who live only for their pay day.

One of the sub plots from the movie "Darna Mana Hai" that comes to mind when I think about government offices is the one featuring Saif Ali Khan. The story begins with Saif checking into a hotel after which the owner of the hotel, Boman Irani, refuses to let him leave. Saif tries his best but to no avail. In the end, he joins Boman in his sinister design to prevent people who check in from checking out. It's bizarre but doesn't it sound like the environment of a government employee's office?

Once in a while, the government is shaken up by movements such as those lead by Anna Hazare and Arvind Kejriwal who are brave individuals. They're trying to clean the rot in the system. At the same time, it's too early to know whether such initiatives will fail or succeed. The system will get to them eventually. Who knows, in some time we may hear that Kejriwal has taken graft in order to fail in his initiative. Everyone seems to want to maintain status quo and safeguard their precious and puffed-up backside. Who can we blame in such a scenario?

When the government does something and fails, it gets crucified by the likes of Anna and Kejriwal. If government decides not to do anything, Anna Hazare is happy but the nation bleeds due to this indecision. The question is, does anybody care for what happens to our nation? I hope with the new government and a once-in-a-century leader like "Narendra Modi", things will change for the better. In fact, from where things stand today, we can only go up.

Are private employees happy?

In private employment, you have to show results commensurate with your pay. Here you can't talk about labour pains, you have to deliver the baby. Someone's money is at stake unlike the government's money, which belongs to everybody and nobody at the same time.

A private employer, most of the times, but not all the time, knows that his success depends on the happiness quotient (HQ) of his employees and hence tries to give them many opportunities for growth—position wise and money wise.

Indian corporates today have designations like "Chief People's Officer". This was unheard of earlier. Now businesses have also started paying heed to the fact that they need motivated employees to deliver on their business numbers. Motivation is nothing but "a motive for action". When you don't have any motive or reason for excelling in a particular job, why would you do it? When companies say, *"Our employees are demotivated,"* who is to be blamed? Employees or employers? Employers have to take the blame as their real job is to make sure their human resource is happy and has some targets to work towards.

The main job of any organization is to align the personal goal of employees to the larger business goals of the organization.

This is the most important point that I am trying to discuss here. This can change the fortunes of many companies who are struggling to stay afloat in today's cut-throat business world.

Organizations have to first understand the aspirations, needs and wants of their employees and have a plan that they disseminate to all employees, which encourages them to achieve the business targets of the organization. When this is done effectively, employees will automatically inch towards their personal goals.

For example, if the organization gives me a business target of Rs 100 crores, I won't be motivated to work hard. For me it is just a number and from the bottom of my heart, I hardly care if it is achieved or not. If it is achieved, I will hog the credit. If not, the best thing to do is to blame everyone around—the market, the company, the boss, the recession, the government, the weather, etc. The horse that kicks cannot pull and the horse that pulls will never kick.

If, for example, an organization links my personal goal of say having enough money for my daughter's education expenses and marriage to its corporate goal of successfully concluding business worth Rs 100 crores, I will have a motive for action and I will move heaven and earth, to achieve that goal.

Organizations that are successful in doing this are successful in their business objectives.

A few organizations in the USA have given their employees the opportunity to preserve their embryos in cryostorage so that they can conceive their child later, when they are ready.

Reliance Industries Limited, had a meeting some time ago to restructure their Human Resource (HR) policies and make them more aligned to the welfare of their employees by providing things like six months of paternity leave, among other things.

Ajay Devgan's HR policy

In one of his interviews, actor Ajay Devgan said that every member of his staff had stayed with him since his first movie (Phool aur Kaante) and had worked with him for more than

20 years. That's what a good/ perfect employer is all about. I imagine his staff must not be considering their work as tedious. They probably enjoy the profile and at times probably do some work for free. We reach a stage in our corporate career when we can carry out our job responsibilities with same dedication and intensity without even being paid for it. This is the stage at which an employee is performing optimally and any employer who succeeds in doing this must be commended. Employers should strive to achieve this stage, only then will they be truly successful in the marketplace.

Waman Hari Pethe: a sharp strategy or the complete lack of any plan?

In the month of June in the year 1994, I went to a Waman Hari Pethe shop in Girgaum, Mumbai. I wanted to buy a gold ring; my first gold purchase since the time I was born. I went inside and looked around in search of the ring counter. Nobody attended to me and moreover, the staff looked at me as though I had come to buy one lakh worth of gold with Rs 10 in my torn pocket. Luckily I found the glass table under which the rings were kept. I asked for one, the sales guy disinterestedly picked it up and kept it in front of me. His gaze seemed to imply that the ring was something I couldn't afford even if I were allowed to pay for it in 100 installments with zero percent interest. I ignored that dog and asked for another ring. He suspiciously picked up the first ring, which was on the table, put it back and then showed me the next one. I realized that he was allowing me to look at only one ring at a time. By then I felt insulted; it was as though he was passing urine on my legs while whistling and laughing at me. I cursed him, in my mind of course, and went out. Then I went to Kemps Corner, which has several jewelry shops. I went into one shop and was greeted by a plump sales girl who seductively asked me what I was looking for. Her gaze suggested that apart from all the gold items, I could also take her wherever I wanted to (that too for free!), provided I buy something first. I asked to see the rings. She ignored my request. Instead she thrust a straw in a cold, fizzy bottle of "Thumbs Up" and gave it to me as if she was offering her modesty to me. I was under pressure. I felt that I had to buy something from here as she had already done me a favour by giving me a cold drink. I thought that if I didn't buy from here, she would feel bad, so I mentally decided to do so. Actually I had gone there to buy a ring for my "would be wife" but here I was more concerned about the feelings of this "would be nobody". Anyway, she showed me some flashy and expensive rings. I liked a few but I didn't like their price tags, rather, my purse protested on seeing the price tags. I finally found something that appealed to me both in terms of looks and price and was considering buying it when suddenly the singer Nitin Mukesh, in all his 200 kg glory, entered the shop. I wonder why the children and grandchildren of Mukesh are still feeding on his goodwill. They shamelessly use his name. I don't think anybody would have even given a chance to Nitin Mukesh, the spent singer or Neil Nitin Mukesh, the bad actor, if it weren't for this name. Although I have to give credit where it is due and admit that I did like Neil in "Kaminey". But I also credit Vishal Bhardwaj for that performance as it appears as though he can even get a wooden stick to act and win a Filmfare Best Actor Award.

To cut a long story short, I bought the ring by that witless but seductive salesgirl only to be told by my family that it was only 18 carats. The one being sold by "Waman Hari" was 23 carat. It was then that I came to know why the girl was treating me like a naked Hrithik Roshan.

The point is, "Waman Hari Pethe" were selling the best product in the industry and hence they didn't require catchy marketing. They didn't have competition earlier and hence could relax without the compulsions of customer management. But now that they have broken into two companies, (whether the split was between father and son or between two brothers, I am not aware and I don't even care) their customer care seems to have improved. The customer has been the biggest beneficiary of this split.

Employees should be made to feel like owners

NRN used to say that if one desires greater success in any venture, they must have entrepreneurs working under them.

A close friend who runs a small business of media related activities once asked me why his employees were not interested in the welfare of the company when he gave them everything: their salaries on time, annual increments, night overtime food allowance, compensatory off the next day for night work, etc.

The reason I gave him was that even though he was giving them all the facilities he was not giving them the feeling of being owners of the company. They needed to feel as though the company's success was their success. Creating such a sense of ownership is very delicate and borders on being a risky proposition. Still I believe that such a work atmosphere is empowering and yields better results.

When they take a decision that, even as a boss you would not approve of, you have to let it go so the employee feels respected and starts feeling and treating the organization as his own. Then he starts working like an employer. He/ she works for the bottom line and stops working for money alone.

If you have an employee who works for money alone, he will not be a great asset to you and will probably say *"Ta, ta!"* to you if and when he gets a better salary.

When someone works for you, he will not quit because he won't get the opportunity to work with a person like you anywhere else. Ajay Devgan's staff could probably get a better salary and/ or perks elsewhere but they will not get an employer like "Ajay" anywhere else. By the way, his real name is "Vishal".

SME employers should be transparent, trusting and impartial.

"Jai Veeru" internal customer/ "Gabbar" external customer:

In the film "Sholay", Thakur's primary aim was to take revenge against Gabbar. Thakur wanted to capture Gabbar alive at any cost. He gets two employees, Jai and Veeru and he makes sure that they are kept happy and motivated so that they continue their mission to capture the dangerous "Gabbar Singh". Jai and Veeru are more than employees, they are Thakur's only means to succeed in his quest. This is because he is an old man and both his arms have been cut-off by Gabbar as a final act of humiliation. On listening to Thakur's story, Jai and Veeru refuse to take any money from him and still promise to carry out his work. This is the kind of feeling that an employer should generate in all his employees. On a lighter note, I am not advocating that you cut off your hands as that will lead to hygiene issues. Not everyone is fortunate enough to have a man Friday—Ramlal—like Thakur did.

In a nutshell what I am trying to say is that you must make sure you consider the interests of your employees as part of your business strategy. They will reward your consideration with loyalty and by taking an active interest in the growth of the organization.

Make sure you treat all your colleagues well as they can help or harm your chances of getting to the next level in the corporate ladder of success.

Happy ascent!

❑❑❑

"The Golden Formula :: 70:20:10"

Please get the above mentioned ratio tattooed on your hand, in the same place where Amitabh Bachchan had his tattoo in the movie "Deewar".

This ratio refers to the time allocation matrix, which you must try to follow, when you are with your customer.

70: Customer talks

20: You ask

10: You tell.

If you follow this simple matrix, sales will follow you.

But it is very difficult because YOU believe (and it's true as well), that you are a good salesperson. If you talk a lot, with finesse, with fine manners, accent, impeccable English, etc., the customer gets impressed but that's about it. Our main objective is not only to impress the buyer but also to get our objective achieved. Our objective here is to sell the product, service or idea, which we have come to meet him for.

Most of the world believes that a good talker is a good salesperson or a good business man. Nothing can be farther from the truth. To say that a good talker is a good seller is nonsense. The smart salesperson just listens.

Why does a good sales guy listen? Selling is converting needs (hidden/ explicit) into wants. As simple as that. I am mentioning selling here but this formula applies to all walks of life. You sell every moment. Whether you are aware of it or not, is secondary. Like we are breathing every moment, whether we are aware of it or not.

In the consumerist world we live in where every moment a person is being bombarded with different sales messages, the word "selling" has almost become a bad word. As a profession, sales is not held in high esteem. This makes me laugh because the truth is that we all sell, every moment we live, we try to sell—our ideas, our opinions, our decisions, etc.

People look down upon selling as a profession because it involves a lot of rejection. Selling is a business of rejections. Even a good salesperson, meets about ten odd prospective clients, until one of them finally says "yes". People look at these nine rejections and treat this profession like the plague. I deliver lectures to management colleges and ask the smart young generation of business students to work in sales for two to three years and then move on to any profession. A good salesperson will always succeed in any profession. But any successful person in another profession may not succeed at sales. Selling involves rejection. This rejection is treated as a personal rejection. It is taken personally. That is the biggest crime. When I go out to sell X company's products, I am not

Sanjay or Vinay or Govind, I am just the salesperson of that company. When a customer accepts the product/ service/ idea, they are not accepting "you". When they reject the product/ service/ idea, they are not, for God's sake, rejecting "you", they are rejecting the company or maybe there are some other reasons which may not relate to you as a person. Those reasons may relate to you as a professional though. For example, if a customer likes your product but he doesn't like you, meaning he doesn't like the way you present yourself, your manners, your dressing or he questions your integrity/ honesty, he will still not do business with you.

In this scenario, where the customer finds something lacking in you, you should move heaven and earth to remove this lacuna from your life.

Ages ago, Dilip Kumar, Naushad and Lata didi were travelling to Malad in a local train. On the way to the studio, Naushad introduced Lata to Dilip saab and said, *"This girl sings very well and I am going to get all my songs from her"*. Dilip asked Naushad to tell him her name again. On hearing the name, he said, *"She is Maharashtrian and will have a heavy Marathi accent when she sings Hindi/ Urdu songs."* Those days all the Hindi songs were full of Urdu words unlike today's songs, which go *"Beedi pike nukkad pe wait tera kiya re, khali peeli athara (18) cup chai bhi toh piya re. Raja beta banke maine jab sharaat dikhayi, tune bola hat mawali, bhav nahi diya re. ABCD pad li bahot, thandi aahe bharli bahot, acchi baate karli bahot, ab karoonga there saath gandi baat, gandi gandi gandi gandi gandi (5 times) baat"*. I shudder to even think what would have happened if such lyrics were shown to Lata didi, what would her reaction have been?

Though on a lighter note, if you observe closely, the songs in that era were equally erotic but the words used were very subtle and soft, which is a hallmark of Urdu as a language. The lines for one such song is as follows: *"Dil joh na kah saka, wahi baat kahne ki raat aayi"*. This line implies a similar meaning but gandi baat is too direct.

Anyways, the main point of the discussion here was regarding Dilip saab's comment on Lata didi's Marathi accent. When Dilip Kumar showed the lacuna (real or perceived, is not known), Lata didi took it positively. If somebody criticises us, we are faced with two options. Either we curse the guy and question whether he has the authority to say something like this. If we feel he does not, then we angrily wonder why the hell he is making demands of us. This approach is self-killing. Feedback is the breakfast of champions. We cannot pat our own back just as we cannot kick ourselves. Hence there are other people who criticize us. We should take it positively and use the opportunity to improve ourselves.

What did Lata didi do after this stinging criticism? She hired an Urdu teacher for three months. She took Urdu diction training from him and then sang a few songs for Naushad. Naushad made Dilip (Yusuf bhai) listen to those songs without telling him that it's the same Lata. Dilip was mesmerised and said that judging by the divine voice he was listening to, the singer must be a Muslim or an Urdu speaker. Naushad then revealed Lata's identity. To his credit Dilip accepted very graciously that he was wrong and he has been a fan of Lata since then. One more relation took birth that day. Dilip saab started calling Lata Mangeshkar, Lata didi. Till date Dilip treats Lata with utmost respect and love, befitting a real sister.

So coming back to our main point, which pains me personally, which is that a lot of people look down upon sales guys. They face a lot of rejection, they are under constant pressure to achieve their targeted sales volumes. My humble request to all of you is that when any sales guy comes to your office, residence or anywhere, the least you can do is treat him with respect. His blessings will make your life a heaven. His curses can also drag you to hell. So be careful...

When the lawyer is arguing his client's case in court, what is he doing? Selling his client's point-of-view so that the judge buys it and gives him a favourable verdict.

When the husband wants to have an afternoon nap and his wife wants to go shopping and he is trying to make an excuse about not going, what is he doing? Selling his point-of-view. Most of the times a husband is not able to sell his idea here as he grudgingly has to go for shopping and create a big hole in his pocket.

When a mother is trying to convince a small child to eat or go to school, what is she doing? She is selling. But, in this case most of the time, a child turns out to be a tough nut to crack and will not buy your idea. In this case, the way the idea is being sold is very crude, direct and it reeks of arrogance on the part of the parent. Most of their negotiations begin with, *"If you don't do this, I will do this or that"*. This is pure blackmail and the child resents it. If you possess good selling skills, you will make the child do what you want him to do at the same time the child will own that idea, which you put in front of him. Now do you see what I mean? In general, parents who negotiate badly also make bad salespersons. They are not able to sell the idea of "doing something", to the child. The child doesn't buy their idea and they push it down his throat, forcefully. It may seem crude, but I must mention it. It is like when someone approaches a girl for marriage and she refuses them. The guy is not able to convey/ sell the benefits of spending the rest of her life with him and in frustration, he rapes her.

Selling is an art, which will make the other guy do the thing you want him to do and feel that he always wanted to do that thing anyway.

Most of the time when we fail to sell something, the reason is only one, which is that as a salesperson, you are not aware of the needs of the client. Any and every living being has a problem. Only dead bodies don't have problems.

When we meet somebody to sell our product/ service/ idea, first try to find out what are the problems he is facing in his life currently. Then with complete honesty, find out how your product/ service/ idea will help him, solve his problem. Then make the client ask you for the solution to his personal problems. It is not easy. You can't expect someone to first open up to you about his problems and show you his weaker side and then ask you for a solution. Asking for solutions seems to betray his lack of control on his own life.

All the things mentioned above, like persuading a client to open up with his innermost problems and asking for the solution from you, is absolutely easy and possible. It is easy and possible only and only if you follow the formula mentioned in this chapter's title.

It takes loads of patience to listen to someone and not only listen but put two-and-two together and guess the nature of the problem, he is facing. Then it takes a lot of character and empathy from a sales guy towards the client, for the client to be able to accept the problem he is facing and ask you for the solution.

A salesperson sells features and a businessman sells benefits.

Even the letters used in the words LISTEN and SILENT are exactly the same.

Begging is required when you have not offered a solution to the customer. Beggars beg you to give them money even though they have done absolutely nothing for you. They show the child in their arms and ask for alms.

In much the same way, when a sales guy does not give a solution, he begs by talking about his potential job loss, family to feed, etc. The beggar is talking about his benefits and wants someone else to pay for this. Hence he has to beg. It is pure begging.

A sales guy is not able to give solutions if he doesn't know the problem. He doesn't know the problem as he has spoken for 95% of the duration of the meeting and the customer has hardly opened his mouth except may be for yawning.

The customer's mouth is similar to his purse. If you allow him to open his mouth as much as possible, he will also open his purse to buy your product/ service.

Dentists and good salespersons, will make you open your mouth and then they fix the problem as they see the problem.

A customer is expressing his emotions when he is talking for quite a length of time. In sales, people seek to prove the logic of buying the said product. But the cardinal rule in sales is—logic can only open the mind of the customer but only emotions can make him open his purse/wallet.

To be honest, there is nobody in this world who is particularly excited to listen. Listening is a great art and is a doorway to many successes in life. But we don't listen, we hear the other person and while he is talking, we are mentally preparing our answer.

It is said that the definition of listening to some people is, 'Waiting for my turn to talk'.

This reminds me of one of the interviews given by Chetan Bhagat for a television channel. He was talking about the time he spent in the Indian Institute of Technology (IIT) and how he had gone to a company for a summer project. There he found some technical issue/ problem, which was going on for years but nobody was able to fix it. One evening, he sat with one of the workers and the worker talked about his life, kids, joys, sorrows, etc. Bhagat listened patiently for more than three hours. The next day, the same worker came up to Bhagat and gave him the solution for the problem which was plaguing the factory for quite some time. He told Bhagat that he wants him to get some good grades in his on-the-job training. Why? Because, he said, *"Nobody in the world has sat with me for three hours, listening to my issues"*. He felt obliged to help Bhagat. Most people treat another person's serious issues as a non-issues and their own non-issues as a matter of life and death.

In the same interview, Bhagat said *"I am not technically inclined (he is an IIT engineer) but I am more of a people's person."* No wonder he got into the Indian Institute of Management-Ahmedabad later, which deals with "marketing" which is actually nothing but a strategy to tackle patterns of human behaviour.

Basically all the business problems we have, are people's problems and not business problems. Most of the so called business brains spend a lot of time and money in trying to treat the symptoms (trying to sort out business issues, unsuccessfully, most of the time) but in reality, they should have treated the disease that is the human mind issues, employees' issues, etc.

If you closely look at the word Business, U comes first, before I; one should take care of U (internal/ external), i.e. the customer, before he takes care of I, i.e. himself.

If you take care of your people, your people will take care of your business. But unfortunately, people go the opposite way and suffer the red ink of business.

Vineet Nayar, former CEO of HCL, has very smartly captured this in the very title of his book, Employees First, Customers Second: Turning Conventional Management Upside Down.

A big firm once gave a group photo of their employees to be printed in the company's advertisement material instead of professional models. That did wonders to the morale of the people along with the wonders it did to the company's bottom line.

In business, all the technicalities are scientific in nature except for one—the very rarest of rare arts, i.e., the art of listening.

Law of Averages + Listening = Success in sales

The Law of Averages always works. The Law of Averages may be bigger or smaller for people depending on their listening skills. If you can't listen, that skill turns into kill (it kills your sales pitch).

Listening is the essential ingredient in all relationships, not only in professional ones but in personal ones as well.

What is the spelling of LOVE?

No, it is not L O V E, it is 'T I M E'.

You love the people who you choose to spend the most amount of time with.

When I see someone talking on the phone, and I observe that he is actually in a hurry to disconnect, he will say things like, *"Haan, haan, ok, ok, I will do it, ok, ok, bye, mein bahut busy hoon, chal bye"*. No prizes for guessing that he is talking to wife, his own wife.

If he was talking to someone else's wife or his girlfriend, he has all the time on the earth. He will whisper sweet nonsense into the phone, asking her what dress she is wearing, what she had for lunch, and other such meaningless questions. He has lots of time for this woman, hence he has love for this woman.

He doesn't have love/ time for his very own and only, wife. Sad, but true.

This applies to both husband and wife.

When a husband goes home and tells his wife that he wants

to tell her something interesting that is happening in his office and his wife, least interested in her hubby's office nonsense, makes some excuse and vanishes into the kitchen, then she is doing the same thing. No time/ no love.

The moral of the story is: Give time and the love is given.

In the movie Jaanbaaz by Firoz Khan, starring Anil Kapoor and Dimple Kapadia, etc., there is a song titled, "Pyaar Do, Pyaar Lo". I think the wordings should be changed now to "Time Do, Pyaar Lo".

In a customer situation, it is not only love which gets communicated, it the respect which you display towards the customer, which gets communicated. When you respect the customer, he will in turn respect you, obey you and make sure that he endows you with what you want, i.e. business. Right?

I will close this chapter on a lighter note, a dialogue from the movie Bhool Bhulaiyya by the talented Priyadarshan, starring 'Khiladi' Akshay Kumar and 'Silk' Vidya Balan.

In that movie, Akshay says, *"Agar tum aurat ko izzat doge, who apni izzat tumhe degi"*.

I am digressing from the main subject but let me put this thought which has been in my mind for a few years into print. The thought is *"Man gives love to get sex and a woman gives sex to get love"*.

This reminds me of a story:

Once an eight-year-old son asked his dad, *"Papa, you are working in a good company. You must be getting a good salary? Can you tell me how much you earn in an hour?"*

The dad, as usual, was not happy with this question and got a bit irritated and asked the son to mind his own business (i.e. studies) and leave these money matters to him.

After some time, the dad felt sorry for his own impulsive and rude behaviour towards his own kid. He goes to his room and says *"Beta, sorry about my outburst a few minutes back. You deserve to know how much I earn. After all, I do it for you son! I earn about Rs 1,000 per hour."*

The son reached into his piggy bank, took out all the coins and started counting. The dad tried to intervene but the kid was too engrossed in counting. Dad kept quiet. After a hectic ten minutes of counting and recounting the son was looking visibly sad. His dad asked, *"What's the matter?"*

The son says, *"Papa, can you lend me Rs 300?"*

His dad replies, *"Yes beta, but why do you require Rs 300?"*

The son says, *"Dad, I have Rs 700 saved from last few days of saving, I need Rs 300 more, so that I can buy 1 hour of your time."*

The dad had tears in his eyes.

He was running around in circles for the kid but the kid remained inside, at the centre of the circle, hardly met or being heard by his own dad.

If we don't have time for our children when they are young, when will we have the time (may be after we turn 60)? You have missed their childhood and no amount of money can get that back. To be in your children's memory tomorrow, you have to be in their lives today.

This incident throws light on this principle of listening, which applies to corporates as well as to the home front. Have a great work-life balance. First put life in your work and both will get balanced automatically.

The moral of this chapter is: Pay attention and listen and you will laugh all the way to the bank.

❑❑❑

"Getting an Appointment"

Speak to any salesperson and he/ she will tell you that the biggest hurdle in their careers is getting an appointment. If anyone can manage this aspect of sales, he can be rest assured that he will clinch the sale.

Like when you are addressing a big gathering, the initial moments with the audience are very crucial. If you cannot connect with the audience in the beginning, the whole presentation goes over their head. Like in the movie "Dil Chahta Hai" when Aamir Khan's character goes to the podium in a pub and says *"Hello, hello, 1 2 4, 1 2 4, arre yeh mike leak ho raha hai kya? 3 kaha hai?"* . This witty statement makes the audience smile (puts them at ease) and the ice is broken.

Similarly, when you are talking to somebody on the phone to ask them for an appointment, you need to try and say something atrocious, shocking or amusing. Yes, you read it right. In today's business world only innovation prevails, "being normal" is boring. As they say in the news media, no news is good news because the only thing that qualifies as news is something that is shocking. Normal is considered boring and people will not give their precious attention to what is normal. By normal I mean something which is expected to happen anyway. Why would anybody bother to pay special attention to it?

Similarly when you approach a prospective customer, you have to try to standout as much as you possibly can.

On August 1, 2014, Rajkumar Hirani gave a full page advertisement for his upcoming film "PK" in the print media across India. This advertisement showed Aamir Khan, in his original form, like the way he was when he was born, stark naked. He had covered his private parts by holding a "two-in-one" radio in front of him. If that radio was not there, his private parts would no longer have remained private but nearly all of womankind (and a small section of mankind) would have feasted their hungry eyes on them.

The art of saying something shocking (Don't get worried, I will explain what I mean by shocking later), is to say it with total conviction. The other person may not believe what you are saying initially but when they hear the commitment and conviction in your voice they feel compelled to listen to you further. The real reason why they are listening to you is to find out why you are so convinced about what you are saying.

Now that you have the attention of that person, who is on other side of phone and for all you know, may be having a romantic/sexual encounter with someone at that very moment, the next thing to do is to make a statement that pulls them out of their environment and compels them to listen to you, not just hear you (which happens on most telephonic calls).

A classic example of taking an appointment with a High Net-worth Individual (HNI) is seen in Amitabh Bachchan's super-hit movie "Trishul" very ably directed by Yash Chopra and written by the greatest Hindi film writing duo of all times "Salim and Javed Akhtar". In a scene from the movie, when Amitabh is trying to meet the elusive R K Gupta, he comes into contact with his receptionist, played by Rakhee. The scene begins with him opening the door and walking upto Rakhee.

Amitabh: Mujhe R K Gupta se milna hai (I want to meet Mr. R K Gupta)

Rakhee: Kya naam hai aapka? (What is your Name?)

Amit: Vijay .... Vijay Kumar

She flips through her appointment diary, doesn't see his name there and says,

Rakhee: Mr Gupta se milne ke liye pehle se waqt lena padta hai (You need prior appointment to meet Mr. Gupta)

Amitabh: Lekin main R K Gupta se abhi milna chahata hoon. (But I want to meet Mr. R K Gupta, "Now")

Rakhee: Woh is waqt bohat busy hai. (He is very busy now)

This is typical of any secretary. He may be busy with her geography, her assets, for all you know.

Now for the shocker which I was talking about.

Amitabh: Kya woh itne busy hai ki us aadmi se bhi nahi mil sakte jo unka lakhon ka fayda kar sakta hai? (Is he so much busy that he cannot even meet a person who can make him a profit of few lakhs?)

The receptionist is shocked. Disbelievingly she asks...

Rakhee: Kya kaam hai aapko? (What work do you have?)

Now please note how she comes down from saying the *"boss is busy"* to saying *"Kya kaam hai apko?"*

Most sales guys fall into this trap and explain everything to the lady (I can't blame them. The way most secretaries talk, with a heavy dose of passion, could make even Anna Hazare guilty of not marrying in his hay days).

Amitabh: RK Gupta se kahiye ke main unhe milna chahta hoon. (Tell Mr. R K Gupta that "I" want to meet him.)

He doesn't fall into Rakhee's trap as he knows Yash Chopra will make her romance with him after a few reels and in a few movies after this one as well.

This is how a salesperson overcomes their biggest hurdle to gaining an appointment with an HNI client—the secretary.

The other option which I have applied many times with great success and also at times, with great embarrassment (details after few pages, hold your guns) is as follows.

I used to call the landline numbers of prospective HNI clients and say *"Give the line to Aamir please"*. I often cold call the offices of top heroes (Unfortunately this trick of mine didn't work with Aamir's receptionist).

Around 99 out of 100 times the person who listens to this careless order about giving the phone to her boss, feels that this person must be very close to him/ her and sometimes transfers the call even without asking the name of the caller.

Now to describe the embarrassing incident I was talking about earlier. Once I was reading the Times of India and I happened to read an article about a senior manager (similar to a CEO in position) whose name I noted and called his landline (as I was already following one sales case there without any luck) and in my usual style asked the receptionist to give my call to Mr Saxena (name changed). Saxena came on the line.

Let me give you a little background information to this story. I used to work with Godrej then, selling copier machines and Saxena worked for Pepsi. When I explained the purpose of my call to him, he listened with deafening silence for a few seconds and then said that *"If I want to sell Pepsi to Godrej, I won't go to Adi Godrej"*. He meant that this particular purchase responsibility was way below his profile. To cut the long story short, be aggressive but attack where it will bear fruits, don't shoot in the dark and expect results.

Sadly, I lost this particular order to a competitor. Not all your strategies will work all the time. Be prepared to take a few knocks along the way to success.

To summarize, you need to start your conversation with a prospective client with a statement that will make him/ her remember you. Don't be afraid to be scandalous (when, for example, talking about the benefits which the customer will receive on meeting you).

Let us first understand all the ways in which you benefit in such a scenario. When something is sold, what do people actually buy? People don't buy a product; they buy the things the product can do for them. When you buy a car, what do you buy? Just a vehicle to transport you from Place A to Place B? If that is the case, you might as well make do with a very old car which only starts with a dhakka (push). When you buy a car, you buy the comfort of going from point A to point B. You also buy the convenience with which you can do things. The higher the degree of convenience, the more the value of the car. If a person had to buy a car just to be mobile, they could go to a scrap yard and bring home any piece of metal, which must have been called a car once upon a time.

People buy the comfort which they perceive that your product/ service gives them. This perception matrix has to be created and sold by the sales guy without any difficulty.

It is said that whenever you buy anything, you pay a price and you receive value. Value is the perceived benefits of a product that a customer has in mind at the time of making a purchase.

When we are selling something whose utility is known to all like a car, you don't have to worry much because a customer by virtue of knowing the product already calculates its benefits in his mind without your knowledge.

But when you sell something whose utility is not very clear to the customer one has to adopt ingenuous ways in which to make the customer aware as demonstrated by "Salim-Javed" in "Trishul".

When Amitabh Bachchan calls R K Gupta and Gupta refuses to give him an audience, he uses one of his tactics. He shows the benefit to Gupta on the phone. Benefits are generally intangible. When I buy a car, the comfort which I get is an intangible benefit. But for you to conclude a business deal quickly, you need to make that benefit work for you. You need to connect the benefit with what the customer values. This is when you will begin to monetize the benefits of your product.

If the word "monetize" alarms you then don't worry. Imagine that you are sitting in a seminar hall with the capacity to seat 500. You are talking to your audience with great enthusiasm and your audience has their heart in their mouth and can't wait to find out what you have to say next. In this scenario you have succeeded in monetizing your ideas, in other words, you are making money from your ideas. The benefits of your product should be such that the customer should need it and be curious about procuring/ purchasing it.

Most tele-calling scripts suggest that you talk to your customer politely.

I would like to differ on this point. You need to be aggressive and take the risk of sounding rude. Yes, you read it right— rude. Because strength respects strength.

Abdul Kalam was once asked about his love for making nuclear missiles. See how the words love and making appeared together in the last line describing a bona-fide bachelor like Abdul Kalam. Kalam, as the whole world is aware, was a very kind-hearted and peace-loving gentleman. And yet he was one of India's foremost authorities on the creation of nuclear missiles which can wipe out entire generations of humanity with the press of a button. This reminds me of a story that somewhat echoes that of Kalam's. There was once a man who used to make bombs. One fine day, by mistake a newspaper reported that he was dead and the caption to this story was that the man who invented the X bomb is dead. This deeply disturbed the man. Not just because people thought he was dead but also because his greatest achievement was the creation of a weapon that took so many lives. At that moment he decided to stop creating bombs (though the merchant of death continues to wreck people's lives even today) and start something related to peace on planet earth. He poured all his energy and resources into peace-loving initiatives, so-much-so that today, the world's most famous award for work that promotes peace in the world was named after him. The name of that gentleman is "Alfred Nobel". Today we see people of various hues and colours receiving the Nobel. Makes one think. Irrespective of what you are today, you can reform yourself if you really wish to; you can make the whole world remember you for all the good work you did.

Coming back to what we had said earlier about being aggressive at the risk of sounding rude, it is important to note here that it is important not to offend your client. Verbal hurt lingers for a long time. A wound is inside your mouth heals very fast but a wound inflicted by an organ inside your mouth, i.e. your tongue, never heals. Hence I advise you to use words carefully because two things once lost can never be retrieved—time and words spoken in haste. On a lighter note, even tooth paste once out of the tube cannot be put back.

Once in an interview, Kalam was asked why, despite being such a peace-loving and soft human being, he chose to make nuclear missiles. Kalam's answer left a deep impression on me. He said *"Strength respects strength"*. He said that if his country had a nuclear missile, the neighboring country would think a thousand times before using nuclear weapons on us as they know we will retaliate. I don't think we need 'nukes' to wipe-out our enemy neighbors. If all 1.28 billion of us decide to relieve ourselves in the direction of their country, they will drown. Jokes apart, I am not in the favour of fights of any kind as any war only brings tears, misery and pain to all the parties concerned. Even the victorious are not happy as they have sacrificed many of their men in the process. God made land but people made boundaries.

This became clear to me on hearing the lyrics to Javed Akhtar's song in the movie "Border". For the first time in the history of Indian cinema, the audience instead of trooping out as soon as the film ended, waited and watched the entire song with complete involvement. The song talks about the futility of the war for all the people involved. In that movie, India wins the war against Pakistan but loses virtually all her soldiers. Sunny Deol is the last man standing but he cannot enjoy his victory as he thinks about the brutal deaths of his soldiers. One line in that song which touched my heart and made me realize the futility of war was *"Hum apne apne desho mein, yeh bandooke kyoon bote hai, jab dono hi ke desho mein kuch bhooke bacche rote hai"*. This roughly translates to—why we are planting guns in the soils of our respective countries, when both of our countries have small children crying over the lack of food. If anyone pays attention to this line, he/she will never support war.

Javed Akhtar, with a single line has created an impact that even a thousand words of prose cannot do.

All the above examples only go to reinforce Kalam's statement that strength respects strength. When we call someone for a business appointment, we need to convey the impression that we are on an equal footing with them, i.e., we are as confident about our work as they are. Only then, the person will respect you and grant you an appointment.

When you beg for appointment, you get nothing or you get an appointment with someone who is one big useless fellow in that organization. When you beg him for attention he will unleash his advice and opinions on you and you will end up being "bheja fried".

This particular person will not be the MAN. Let me explain to you why you always need to meet the MAN. All you beautiful ladies out there, please don't get me wrong. What I mean by the MAN is that person in the organization who has the "Money, Authority and Need" for your product.

When you are weak on a tele-call, or too courteous on a call, you tend to fail because the listener has listened to similar sales pitches more than a thousand times today begging him to listen to them, before your call came. You need to be different to get an appointment.

And here I go filmy again:

In the movie Deewar, the younger version of Amitabh polishes boots for a living but believes in himself and above all respects himself a lot. He says, *"Mein bhikh nahi maang raha. Paise uthake do"*. (I am not begging pick up the money & give it to me.) Imagine an eight-year-old boy, whose shirt is crumpled from behind as he has slept on the street wearing the same shirt, a shirt whose pocket is torn and is hanging, who wears a worn-out short pant. This boy is a boot polish boy who is polishing shoes outside Mahalakshmi Race Course in Mumbai. A car of the Mercedes kind pulls up and two suited, booted guys embark and begin discussing which horse they are going to bet on. They come to this small boy and one of them puts his foot in front of him to get it polished. The boy polishes his shoes with complete sincerity and says, *"Ho gaya saab"*. The suited guy throws a coin towards this three-foot-something boy. This is what prompts him to make the previous statement.

What guts, what attitude. You will need a similar attitude when seeking an appointment with an HNI client.

This scene reveals two things--that he loves and respects himself and that he also takes pride in what he is doing. While most of us would equate a boot polish boy with beggar, Jr Amitabh refuses to believe that he is a beggar and demands that he be paid in a respectable way. He wants the money to be given in his hands with utmost respect as this is the compensation he receives for his work for you just as the services of any other service provider such as a barber, cable operator, doctor, etc., who collects charges for the services he provides.

Just as Kareena says in "Jab we met", *"Main apni sabse badi favourite hoon"* (I am the most favourite of myself) you must believe that you are good. Nobody on the planet can deliver this dialogue better than Bebo. When you love yourself the whole world cannot ignore you for very long.

Most tele-callers will teach you to take an appointment by hook or by crook. This is because these tele-marketing executives have targets of how many so called leads they have generated in a day. This is why you will find tele-marketing girls using all their charm to get an appointment from an average looking boy, barely in his 20s who is badly groomed. Now unless the client on the other end isn't straight in his sexual orientation, he will not be happy when faced with the surprise of being visited by a male sales guy when his appointment was taken by a seductive female voice on the telephone.

This is the moment of truth for the poor sales guy. He faces contempt from customer for no fault of his. If the tele-caller is female, customers often say to the tele-caller that if she comes in person, they will take it. By 'it' I mean the product (what a naughty imagination you have). At the end of the day, she is trying to sell the product not herself.

These tele-callers can also be very smart. They say they will come and take an appointment but the poor sales boy (who actually goes for meeting) is the one who has to face the music from customers who take perverse pleasure in ridiculing them.

To summarize my advice on tele-calling:

1. Make sure your opening lines grab the attention of your customer.

2. Make your customer believe that his entire life will change (of course for the better) if he opts for your product/ service. This is something that you must believe too if you want to sound convincing. The belief in your heart goes to his heart, when your words fall on his ears. It is said that "jhoota gale se bolta hai, bhookha pet se and only sachcha dil se bolta hain". This roughly translates to the following—a liar speaks from his throat, a person who is starving speaks from his stomach and a person who is true speaks from his heart.

3. Be aggressive, be arrogant. Yes, you read it right .Your arrogance will seen as a reflection of the quality of the product you sell. Donald Trump was once asked about his arrogance and he said, *"If you are selling gold, you have to be arrogant or else the customer will think you are selling shit"*. Such an attitude can boomerang on you but I believe, *"It is better to die on ones feet than live on ones knees"*.

Love yourself as though you are God's gift to the business and sales industry.

Happy appointment!

10

"Is Sales an Art or a Science? The Law of Averages (LOA) and Listening"

To say that one knows sales techniques is to say that you know how a sale should be consummated. Sales involves two things: the first is to know that rejection is in the DNA of a salesperson. Here's an example from the movie "Company" directed by Ram Gopal Varma. In one scene several friends of a gangster (played by Vivek Oberoi) are getting killed in front of him and this makes him distraught. On seeing his precarious mental condition, an inspector, ably essayed by Mohanlal, a veteran of Malayalee cinema, tells him to take their deaths in his stride. He says *"Yeh tumhare dhande ki jaat hai,"* which means that such a thing is in the DNA of the underworld in which you work. Selling is nothing but a business of rejection. A person who can digest rejection; who can tolerate it but not accept it, will go on to win or clinch coveted deals.

Let us look at the topic of rejection in some detail. When we meet ten people, (depending on which product we are selling, the quality of our salesmanship and the reputation of the company whose product we are selling) may be one will accept our proposal and buy our product/ service. For every ten people that we meet, there's a chance that one person may accept our proposal. This ratio is called the "Law of Average" or LOA. What this means is that out of ten people, nine are rejecting our proposal. This means that 90% of the ten people have refused to buy from us and only 10% are buying from us. A salesperson hears "No" more often than he/she hears "Yes", which is why I said that this was a business of rejection. The ratio of 10:1 just an example to show you how LOA works. Anyone who is in sales has to understand that even if he is a 'cat' in sales, he will have his own LOA. He should be aware of his LOA. How does one become aware of his LOA? By religiously maintaining a daily/weekly/monthly/yearly sales report. When we review this at the end of the month, a pattern begins to emerge in the form of numbers. If the number of people I met is around 100 and the number of sales contracts I have received is 10, then my LOA is 10:1. The beauty of LOA is that if you work consistently, I repeat consistently, then your LOA starts to improve. This means that if you are getting one client after ten meetings and if you keep up your routine without interruptions or breaks, you may get two clients after ten calls a few months later. This could increase to three out of ten, four out of ten and so on. Hence the LOA is dynamic and can improve if you are consistent with your efforts. The reverse is also true. If you are not consistent enough, you might slip to a figure of one client after 11 or 12 meetings. Here the LOA is on a downward spiral.

"Consistency" also plays a dominant role in anyone's success. Anything repeated again and again, regularly, has to yield positive results at some point.

Can you imagine a bucket of plain water breaking a hard rock? Only a fool would think so, right? If you notice carefully, if this same quantity of water is placed in a pot with a small hole at the bottom and this water is allowed to fall from a height at, a regular intervals on a hard rock, eventually it will break.

This is precisely the reason why we offer "bell patra" on the pindi of God Mahadev/ Shankar. In this situation also water or milk is made to fall at regular intervals, which can cause harm to the pindi but when the bell patra is on the pindi the impact of that water/ milk gets reduced significantly and the pindi is safe from any damage.

There is a formula you can follow to achieve results, successful results and that is:

Result = Q1 x Q2

Where Q1 is quality and Q2 is quantity.

When you start with a new product or in a new sales job, the "quality" Q1, of your sales pitch may not be at its highest point. In this scenario, your Q2 or "quantity" should be very high. As you keep at it with fanatical consistency, your "quality" will increase and you may reduce the "quantity" later to get the same results or you may maintain "quantity" at the same high level and reap better results.

So this summarizes the first thing necessary in sales i.e. an understanding that rejection is a part of your job and that your LOA is a dynamic ratio and can improve at any point.

The other most important thing to do is to "listen". In a sales situation, a salesperson should have the self-control to listen. This is very necessary because we can sell anything to anybody only if we know what he/ she wants. No one can sell something to someone if he/ she genuinely doesn't want it. If in this case, you do succeed in selling something then it can only be with the help of cheating, which I strongly oppose. I request all of you to refrain from cheating for your own good. Cheating may give you a "sale" in the short-term but will rob you of a long-term relationship with your client. This honest relationship can result in loyal, consistent sales, which has a lot more monetary value than the initial sale which you make by cheating. It is said that *"Jhoot ki taakat badi hoti hain, umer kam hoti hai."* This means that a lie has massive power but such power is short-lived.

Now we come to the question of whether sales is an art or a science. Even though this question is as old as the story of Adam and Eve, every one you ask will give you a different answer because everyone likes sounding smart. Beware of "pseudo-intellectuals" whose main motto is to oppose the other party's opinion. They take great pride in doing that and actually use all their energy to do so. Opinions are like assholes, everyone has one. So let's not dwell on assholes anymore. I'll let that be the topic of a forthcoming literary masterpiece. Also one should not judge himself only through his past as he may not be living there anymore.

The sales process when conducted with complete control seems like an art. One has to spend a lot of time doing homework, which makes the process look effortless and people think of it as a "work of art".

There was a great pianist in the United States, who used to play the piano like a dream. Once a fan told him *"I would die to be able to play the piano like you."* To this the pianist answered,

"You are right. I did die and only then was I able to play the piano the way I am playing it now."

On the subject of art I would like to ask, what is art? If Salman Khan paints something and it becomes a work of art because he is The Salman Khan, can his painting be counted as art?

Once Salman's house was getting renovated. He saw a few paintings lying on the floor to be hanged on the walls. He had a look at those paintings and found them to be just about okay. He casually asked about their prices to someone and they said it was Rs nine lakhs per piece only. He got the shock of his life. After this, he created a few paintings and people found them better than those nine lakh ones. Salman's mother Salma ("Sushila" before marriage) is a good painter herself and Salman must have received his talent from her because his father, Salim Khan was a different kind of artist; he moved people with his pen. Salman Khan is real superstar, all his recent movies have been monster hits and most of these movies have a paper-thin plot, no story line, no acting talent from the supporting cast—In "Jai Ho", the heroine could not act to save her life, are directed by people near and dear to Salman, such as Atul Agnihotri, Sohail Khan and Arbaaz Khan, among others. They are called directors only because of their proximity to Salman. Despite all this, all of his recent films have been hits. For this there is only one reason, "Salman Khan" himself. He carries the entire movie on his own shoulders without any help from anybody. By mistake he sometimes works with talented directors like Sanjay Leela Bhansali (Hum Dil De Chuke Sanam), Sooraj Barjatya (Maine Pyar Kiya, Hum Aapke Hai Kaun, etc.). I am saying by mistake because after a few months, we read that these directors (with the exception of Sooraj Barjatya, so far at least) have stopped working with "bhai". Even the talented Anubhav Kashyap (Dabang) parted ways with him. Salman seems to have a good heart and a king-size ego.

Due to his golden heart, he wants to help people. This isn't to say that Barjatya, Bhansali or Kashyap require help. They are capable and good in their art. Bhansali can even cast a street dog in his most romantic film and make the dog romance Deepika and the film will be a hit. This is what Sanjay L Bhansali is capable of. He is not at the mercy of the stars but the other way round.

Coming back to the point, which is, why Salman is a superstar. I think it is because he is least bothered about any parameter of movie making except that which concerns himself, unlike Aamir and Shah Rukh Khan. Aamir always takes great pains at making sure that the pre-production for his movies is flawless. He invests a lot of time in understanding the script, locations, co-actors, etc. Shah Rukh mainly relies on the script and above that, on the ability of the director. Most of his movies are directed by successful and capable directors like Yash Chopra, Adi Chopra, Karan Johar, Farah Khan, Rohit Shetty (he is also an able director, made from the same mould as "Manmohan Desai", who used to make the audience believe that one can write the word "mard" with a knife on the chest of a one-day-old child and throughout this ordeal, the child is laughing. Hats off to you Manji, you knew your art and you had rock solid convictions). This quality of Manmohan Desai's conviction, is also of paramount importance when it comes to selling. Customers don't buy the product, they buy your conviction in the product.

Manmohan Desai was once asked about whether he has brains because as all his movies were brain-less hits. He replied, *"Mein dimag se nahi sochta, mein dil se sochta hoon."* This means that I don't think with my head but with my heart. This is the reason why his movies used to touch the hearts of audiences and his movies used to be hits.

In the last scene of the movie "Amar Akbar Anthony", Amar, Akbar and Anthony, played by Vinod Khanna, Rishi Kapoor and Amitabh Bachchan respectively, assemble at the villain's den. The late Mr Jeevan was the main villain in the film and he has been searching for this trio. Now the heroes have come there in disguises so that the villains do not recognize them. But in the songs, they give away their identity by saying *"Ek jagah jab jama ho teenoh, Amar, Akbar, Anthony"* (We have assembled at one place, Amar, Akbar, Anthony). Bachchan raised this concern with Manmohan but the director told him not to worry because Indian people did not look for logic, they wanted magic. He was right and the movie was an all-time hit.

Coming back to Salma, Salman Khan's mother. In the beginning, when Salim Khan was a struggling actor (not writer) he was staying in a flat owned by the villain Ajit in Mahim. Ajit wanted to sell that flat and allowed Salim to stay there till his flat was sold. It was then that Salim met Sushila, a Maharashtrian brahmin girl. Salim was a very handsome man then and even now and Sushila fell in love with him. Before he met Sushila, Salim had two massive heart breaks in Indore but he loved Sushila's simplicity and honesty. They eventually got married against the wishes of Sushila's parents who stopped talking to them till Sohail, their youngest son, was born. Her parents went to see the third born i.e. Sohail and a tearful reunion took place between them and their daughter. There was a period of about five to six years when they were not on talking terms with Salma and Salim. Later when her father got to know Salim better, he used to regret that he had wasted five years without the company of such a gem of a person for no reason.

Salim saab is the personification of kind heartedness. Many of you know the story of a girl named "Arpita". Salim saab used to see a woman on the pavement with a small girl. One day, he saw that the woman had died and the small girl was crying and trying to shake her mother to get her to wake up. The heart-wrenching sight broke his heart; the small girl's entire universe was her mother. She was left with no one in this big bad world. As the dialogue in Mukaddar ka Sikkandar goes, *"Jiska koi nahi, uska khuda hota hai"*(If you don't have anybody, You have God). I think Salim Khan is God. I mean it. He took that small girl home and brought her up better than his own children. I say this because the Khan family never spent a lot of money on the marriages of either of their sons—Arbaaz or Sohail, but they spent a fortune on Arpita's wedding. Salman also takes great pride in loving his sister. Hats off to them. It is people like them that prove that God exists. They say that the proof that God exists is, in the kind deeds of strangers because he does his work through them.

Let's go back to the main topic of whether sales is an art or a science. You may have the talent in you but you may not know it or you may not believe in it. Any act repeated over and over again becomes "perfect" and "perfection" repeated over and over turns into "excellence" and the next step is art. So sales is also an act which can be perfected over a period of time through repetition. The key word here is "repetition".

If you are given a soap to sell, keep on meeting customers. You should initially set a target, not of the number of soaps you will sell, but of the number of people you will talk to about the soap.

Selling is nothing but getting the message across.

If Raju is a great sales guy and Sanju is average. Raju talks about his product to ten guys in a day whereas Sanju talks about it to a 100 people in a single day, who do you think will conclude more sales?

You don't need to be Einstein to answer this one. Sanju will be the winner because there is a science working in the background, not art.

This science is the Law of Averages I spoke about earlier. If you are selling soap and you meet 100 people and sell five soaps, your LOA for soap is 20:1.

If you are selling printers. You meet 100 people and sell two printers, your LOA is 50:1. The lower your LOA the more effective your strategy.

This is the most important but criminally neglected aspect of the science of sales.

For you to calculate your LOA for a particular product, you need to know the number of visits you made to a customer. Religiously capture all the details of your visits in your sales book. After doing this for three months, you will come to know your LOA.

The biggest enemy to the success of any salesperson is a reduction of his/ her enthusiasm level.

LOA is the solution for this drop in enthusiasm. In fact it takes enthusiasm in the opposite direction—northwards or upwards.

Let me tell you how.

When you attend a meeting in the morning with the rest of the sales team you hear all the "gupt gyan" given by your boss or training guy, you become all charged up and are raring to go, meet with people and get new sales. It all seems so easy in a cosy, air-conditioned training room.

When you get out of the office and feel the heat, dust or rain on you, half of your enthusiasm evaporates. You call your colleague on his cell and join him at a tea stall where he is sipping that dirty, hot, coloured water that goes by the name of "cutting chai" in grubby, stained glasses.

After abusing the company, the product, the boss, the economy, the cricket team, Sania Mirza & the country (this list is never ending), you go to make your first call. You meet the customer and he tells you, he has not yet decided what to do or he comes up with some genuine objection and refuses to purchase the product. As a result your enthusiasm goes down further.

In such a scenario, being aware of your LOA will make you happy. In this case, if your LOA is 20, you will know that all you need to do is hear 19 more "NOs" to get your sale. So actually, you are closer to your sale as you have already heard one "NO". In this case you will find that your enthusiasm doesn't nosedive on hearing a negative reply.

You should then enthusiastically go to the next customer and then the next and you will get your order after 20 such calls.

I will tell you of another formula in sales. It's called —"sw, sw, sw, gtn". In sales if one follows this formula, he will always be in bliss. It basically stands for, *"Some will, some won't, so what, go to next".*

Isn't it simple? Yes, this is as simple as going to the bathroom to pee, provided you believe in LOA. You will believe in LOA if you work your ass off for a minimum of three months and also capture all your data in a work book. Study the work book every week, month and quarter and you will arrive at a magical figure as your LOA.

Sales is all about LOA. For a healthy LOA, you need more activity and need to meet different people.

Track the new people/ customers you meet, to calculate your LOA correctly. LOA figures work on new customer visits only and also on follow-up calls.

Follow-up calls are a great waste of time though and any salesperson is only fooling himself (though he feels, he is fooling his boss) by unnecessarily following up with a customer who shows no signs of making a purchase.

When you follow up excessively, you are actually begging a customer to give you the order. Salespeople are not beggars. They provide a solution to the customer that makes his life better and are adequately rewarded for their efforts. Remember the young boot polish boy from "Deewar". I keep coming back to this example because the attitude he shows, even when faced with two people more powerful and stronger than him, should be the attitude of a sales guy.

When you believe you have provided your customer with a product more valuable than the price the customer pays for it, you become a bit arrogant. The customer is happy to see this arrogance in you as he equates your arrogance with the quality of the solution you have just provided him.

It is better to die on your feet than live on your knees. I repeat.

Coming back to the question of follow-ups, consider the following scenario:

You meet a prospective client, understand his situation, concerns, etc. and give him a suitable solution. Please be genuine in your sales and believe in your solution. The solution should be customer-centric and not salesman-centric. We should sell what the prospect wants and not what you want to sell (because of higher sales incentives for a particular product/service).

Focus on you "Mission" and not on your "Commission".

The number "six" when seen from the opposite direction looks like a "nine". 6 & 9...

If a customer sees nine, and you know its six but don't tell him (if you are selfish and a bad salesperson) and the customer senses that you are seeing six and not nine (which is his concern), he loses faith in you. Once you lose the trust of a prospect, you also lose the sale.

If you want to be a good sales man, first be a good man.

When you give an honest solution to a customer, and he thinks for a moment and comes up with a few objections, which you cannot tackle there, you must go back to your office, find a solution and only then come back. This is a justifiable reason for coming back because ultimately your priority is to offer your client a correct solution. If a customer says he will think about purchasing the product, ask him a few more questions. What does he want to think about? What is bothering him about your solution? Ask him why he is not buying your product now and ask him when he will be ready to buy it. You need to understand what is stopping him from buying it immediately. You will get lots of data, which will help you when you make your next call. You need to have the guts to ask such direct questions. You can have the courage, if and only if, you have given him the correct solution and you genuinely believe that by buying your product, he is going to be benefitted immensely.

If you know his objections, then you can call him (on the telephone or meet him in person) to solve his objections with solid facts/ figures/ data and not with, *"Sir, please give me the order or else I will lose my job"*.

When you solve his objections, once again ask him about his previous concerns. Try to find out if your modified solution was able to address them and then ask for the order.

Here's another formula to help you remember what you need to ask your customer:

Customer's situation = WWW

W = why the customer is buying this category of product?

W = why he is buying it from you?

W = why he is buying it this month?

The answer to these three "W"s will give you your prospect's exact situation and you will never go wrong with your sales forecast.

Figure out the hard figures of sales by calculating your LOA in your heart and you will win all sales battles hands down. You will be laughing all the way to the bank then, where you will have a six figure balance.

All the best!

11

"Under commit, over perform"

The basis of trust in any relationship lies in the fulfilment of commitments. If a commitment is not fulfilled, it turns into a false promise or into your inability to take your own word to its logical and pre-decided conclusion.

In the movie Trishul, Vijay (Amitabh Bachchan) promises R K Gupta (Sanjeev Kumar) that he will buy his land for Rs five lakhs while simultaneously admitting that he doesn't have any money. He says, *"Mein aapse paanch lakh ki baat kar raha hoon aur mere paas paanch phuti kowdiya nahi hain"* (I am talking to you about Rs 5 Lakhs but I don't have even Rs 5 with me.). However he gives his commitment to Gupta that he will pay his money in full within 15 days. Vijay does whatever is required and gives Gupta a cheque for five lakhs on the seventh day. That's what I mean by the statement "under commit and over perform". This makes for a great corporate lesson.

In today's corporate world, people are falling over each other to commit the moon, sun and everything in between to their bosses, their customers and all their stakeholders, knowing fully well that they don't have the balls of steel (desperation) required to deliver on that promise. In their minds, they think that even if they deliver 60-70%, the other person will be happy. This is nonsense. When you deliver on your promise, people are happy. If you fall short, people are sad/ upset/ angry. People are delighted when you go beyond your promise. An upset customer may badmouth you to 16 of your prospective clients. A happy customer keeps his mouth shut and doesn't badmouth or recommend you to anyone. A phenomenon that may seem strange but is scientifically tested and proven. A delighted customer on the other hand will talk about you, to a minimum of 26 of your prospective customers.

If one decides to employ this formula of UCOP (Under Commit and Over Perform), he will never be short of business and his business development will be entirely carried out by his delighted customers, absolutely free of cost. In a way, they function like employees doing business for you, without expecting any payment in return. Your payment to them is only in terms of the happiness they feel of getting more than they expected from you.

The first step should be to commit with the aim of fulfilling that promise.

The next step is your quest to delight your customer. Try to achieve your commitment before the stipulated time as Vijay did in "Trishul". When Vijay says 15 days, he very well knows that he can do it in seven odd days, as he doesn't intend to sit on his backside and wait for things to happen. He straight away begins work on the task and tries to make things happen.

After his meeting with Gupta, he goes to Madho Singh, the illegal occupant of Gupta's land, who is running an illegal gambling and boozing den there. Vijay asks him to vacate the land by 11 am tomorrow. Madho Singh hits him. Vijay bleeds from his mouth but holds himself back and says that tomorrow at 11 am, he will come and take possession of the land. Vijay could have attacked Madho Singh then and there. However, as per his plans as well as his ethical beliefs, he feels that it is important to give the goonda a notice period of at least one day. Then Vijay goes to Prem Chopra and asks him to lend him five lakhs against the land which he has just purchased from Gupta. Chopra asks whether the land has been vacated by the goonda because otherwise it is useless to him. Vijay promises him that Singh will vacate the land at 11 am tomorrow. Chopra says that if Singh becomes Mr India (invisible) from the said land, he will lend him five lakhs. The next day at 11 am, Vijay reaches the spot with an ambulance as he doesn't want any of the goondas to be critically injured and to die. His objective is clear. He doesn't want to settle any score with Singh. He just wants to get the land cleared. He does not want to involve the police. In case someone got critically injured, dealing with all the formalities with them would be a big waste of time.

Now there's another lesson to be learnt here from the fight sequence that ensues between Vijay and the goondas. When Vijay enters, all the goondas converge on him but Singh asks them to stand down because he intends to fight him alone. Since Vijay is alone, Singh is not afraid to tackle him alone. Maybe he was being fair or maybe he was being overconfident. Either way he assumes that he will crush Vijay alone. Vijay repays this debt in a few minutes. During the fight, Vijay gets a big wooden rod and goes to hit Singh. He goes near Singh and throws the rod to him and gets another rod for himself as he wants to fight in a fair manner. What character! Even while fighting with someone he keeps his values intact. This quality of fairness quality is forgotten by most corporate chieftains as well as their employees. Only one thing matters today i.e. winning (the bottom line) by hook or by crook, but mostly by crook. It is a sad state of affairs indeed as in this cheating drama the one who suffers the most is the hapless end user, aam (mango) aadmi; people like you and me. Though after the publication and success of this book, I will no longer be an aam aadmi but certainly a bada aadmi, insha allah! I am not joking, I mean it! I believe it! You will see!

There is only a miniscule difference between an ordinary and an extra-ordinary person. In fact, it is that "extra" something which makes an ordinary person extra-ordinary.

If we keep adding something extra/ more to whatever we do in life, we become extra-ordinary. Say you get up at 7 am every day. If you were to get up 15 minutes earlier (just a bit extra) to read some quality literature, you would have read for about 60 mins after four days. Just imagine what so much reading can do to your knowledge! This 15 minutes separates the boys from the successful men. The same thing applies for all other aspects of our lives like our health (wake up 30 minutes early from bed to exercise), our quest for spiritual answers (take another 15 minutes off from some other activity to meditate), etc. To sit calmly (without any thoughts in your mind) is difficult to achieve but not impossible. Doing this can take you from zero to hero. When your mind reaches a state of ZERO, your journey to the state HERO begins. When you sit calmly and thoughtlessly for 15 minutes and at the end of these 15 blank minutes, you wish for anything, I repeat anything (as long as it is for the good of everyone and does not harm anyone), you will get your wish fulfilled. When we are without thoughts, which is our essential state (we were like this before we were born), we are closest to the divine and any wish asked for in such a state is fulfilled by God. God fulfills all our wishes but when you are without thoughts and then you ask for something, God listens to your request. Otherwise he is not even able to hear what you want to say because of the traffic of thoughts in your mind. It's the same as being at a busy train station like "Chatrapati Shivaji Terminus" in Mumbai and seeing your friend going on to the opposite platform; even if you shout his name he will not be able to hear you and he will leave. Similarly, when there are a lot of thoughts crowding our mind, God is not able to hear us.

When the station is empty at 4 am, if you call someone even at the far end of the platform, he will hear you. The same thing happens to the communication between us humans, and God.

Infosys has always stuck to the maxim of UCOP. They were the first company in the Bombay Stock Exchange to start the practice of offering quarterly guidance, i.e. forecasting what their sales, profits etc. will be in the next quarter. In the past 30 years of their existence (Initial Public Offering, June 1992), they have never over committed and underperformed. They always UCOP. N R Narayana Murthy used to say that if he did not know what his company was doing at least for the next three months, he was not fit to be in the business, which is also part owned by many other stakeholders and is not a "lala"company (company of which he is the sole owner).

In a scene from Rowdy Rathore, Akshay Kumar says, "*Mein jo bolta hoon, woh karta hoon*" (I do, what I say). Later in the film his character dies and is replaced by a duplicate who also says, *"Mein jo bolta hoon, woh karta hoon,"* (I do, what I say) and adds in a lighter vein, *"Mein jo nahin bolta, woh toh definitely karta hoon"* (I, definitely do, what I don't say). The second declaration is very detrimental to the interest of all stakeholders in a corporate like we witnessed during the Satyam saga. The second dialogue could have been, *"Joh mein nahin bolta, woh mein delete karta hoon"* (I delete, what I don't say).

There are many people in this world who don't know the "principals of management" as they are taught in management schools like IIM but they unerringly use these principals in their day-to-day business transactions. Take the case of the doodhwala bhaiyya who would come and sell us one litre or one-and-a-half litres of milk, etc. When we used to ask for one litre, he used to give us one liter and then add one small quantity of milk extra. We subconsciously used to value that bit of free milk and appreciate him for it. Though, for all we know, the bhaiyya may have added as much or more water to the milk than the free quantity he gave you.

There was a small girl who used to buy a kilogram of chocolates every month from one particular shop in her neighborhood. Though there were two similar shops, she used to buy only from one particular shop. When her father asked her why she reserved this preferential treatment for one shop, she said it was because the uncle there gave her more chocolates and the other uncle gave her less. The dad was puzzled and went to see for himself. What he saw can be interpreted as a clear and profound management message of "perception being stronger than reality". In fact, "perception is everything". One shopkeeper used to keep about 800 grams on the weighing scale and then add another 200 grams but the other guy used to put more than the entire quantity on the weighing scale and remove the extra, which is why the girl perceived that he was giving her less.

When you go to purchase fish, you will notice that instead of giving you cash discounts the fisherwoman prefers to add a few more small pieces of fish to your bag. The same thing applies to the subziwala (vegetable vendor).

The best salespeople I have ever met are those in Crawford Market or Fashion Street in Mumbai. They can size up a customer vey smartly and will instinctively know about the customer's pocket size (how much money he/ she is carrying), his/ her attitude towards making a purchase, his/ her taste, etc. Then the salesperson will try to manipulate the buyer with the help of the UCOP principal.

I have a Tata car and whenever I face any service issues, I take the car to a Tata authourised service centre in Vashi. The attendant there always sees the problem and quotes at least 30% more than what he knows will be the service charges. I can safely say this because this has been happening with steady regularity for more than four years and hence cannot be a mere coincidence. When he says I may have to shell out about Rs 4,000, I get shocked. Then he says he will check the car thoroughly and then call to give an exact estimate and take my permission before going ahead with the repairs. He then calls after five hours and says that the repair kharcha (expense) is coming to Rs 2,800 and I say "ok" happily under the foolish (on my part) impression that I am getting a good deal. His use of "expectation management theory" where he raised my expectations of the expense and then offered something for a lesser price was a smart strategy.

One of the most neglected and abused strengths of every human is "the spoken word".

It is said that if you speak the truth for 14 years, whatever you speak thereafter will be true; your predictions will turn out to be true. Every spoken word has immense power to change your destiny. Our body is made up of cells and every cell reacts to all the spoken words uttered by us. Words affect our thoughts. Thoughts affect our feelings and feelings are directly connected to the outcome of any action. If you feel positive about something, its benefits will multiply with unfailing accuracy. If you feel bad about not having enough money, you will have to keep on feeling good about having enough money for the next few days or months. Hence, even if you don't have money for your next meal and you still feel good about money, i.e. about having thoughts/ feelings about having lots of money in your pocket/ bank account, you will overcome your deficiency of *"Vitamin M"* and will be awarded with riches, affluence and abundance.

Words once spoken have power over others, if the other party takes them seriously. The other party will take them seriously if you have a history of honoring the spoken word.

When we dishonor our own word, we insult ourselves. When we say we will be somewhere by 11 am and reach only at 11:15 am, we insult ourselves and kill the power of our own spoken word as henceforth your own mind will not take you seriously, forget about the person who is waiting for you, and you will always reach late for meetings. It is a vicious circle.

If you abuse time, time will abuse and ruin you. Respect the spoken word.

Sanjay Gadhvi, the director of the "Dhoom" movie series, said in one of his interviews that the word of Aditya Chopra is worth more than 500 pages of written contract to me. If it is said only to please Adi, who is a big shot in Bollywood then I don't know what to say. But looking at Adi's conduct in the industry, I can safely say that Gadhvi was not making an exaggeration. This is one of Chopra's biggest achievements (even more than the successful "Dilwale Dulhaniya Le Jayenge"). All of us should strive to get people to say similar things about us.

He certainly knows the principal of UCOP as the same principal was advocated strongly in "Trishul" by his very own dad, the greatest maker of romantic movies—Yash Chopra.

Sometimes a result that was committed, is the only thing expected of us, nothing more. The example of this line of thinking is in the movie "Sholay". During the final moments of the movie, when Amitabh dies, Dharmendra goes wild and starts abusing all the gang members by calling them "dogs". He threatens to kill them and drink their blood saying, "Kutte, kamine, mein tera khoon pee jaoonga. Gabbar Singh, main aa raha hoon" (I will drink your blood, Gabbar, I am coming). Then he rides his horse and reaches Gabbar's adda (den). He fights with Gabbar with real vengeance. When he is about to strangle Gabbar with a thick wooden stick, suddenly Thakur Baldev Singh (Sanjeev Kumar) appears from nowhere. Thakur asks Dharmendra to give Gabbar to him, Dharamendra refuses and says, "Nahin, Isne mere dost ki jaan lee hai, main isse jaan se mar doonga" (No, he has killed my friend, I will kill him).

The commitment Jai and Veeru made was that they will hand Gabbar over to the Thakur zinda (alive). Here Dharamendra was exceeding his brief and was trying to over perform by killing Gabbar and making Thakur's job easier. Thakur doesn't like this and reminds Dharam that the commitment of handing over Gabbar to Thakur was made by that same friend who is now no more. On listening to this, Garam Dharam wakes up from his emotional distress, retreats and breaks the thick wooden stick with his bare hands while mouthing one more gem of a dialogue by Salim-Javed. He says, *"Yeh wada mere dost ne kiya hai, isliye. Agar mein kiya hota, toh tod deta"* (I cannot break this promise as it was made by my friend, I would have broken it, if I had made it). And instead of breaking the wada, he breaks that wooden stick; a nice metaphor added by the director.

It is very easy to succeed in the corporate world today. Most people who work for a salary just do things to justify their paycheck. People who UCOP have no competition at all, as you hardly find people in the corporate world, who want to give back much more than what they are paid for. People who do what they are paid for will be successful but for people who over perform, the whole world will stand on their heads to salute them and they will create big records of success, wherever they go.

In addition to this, people who commit to a time at which they will come and reach before the designated time are also following the principal of UCOP. They will also see a lot of success in their endeavors. When one respects time, the world respects them because time itself respects nobody; time waits for no one.

Punctuality is an art of waiting for others

Spiritually speaking, people who operate on this principal of over performance are operating from a different plane, a different level.

Some people operate from a lower self or "jeevatma". They barely give to others compared to what they receive. Some people are always trying to give more than they receive. They operate from a higher self or "paramatma".

When you are operating at a higher self, success and happiness is yours for the taking.

Anyways, in spite of this fetish for performance, we should sometimes stop and look at where we are going. Sometimes, it my so happen that we reach the top of our success ladder and on looking back, we see that the ladder was leaning on the wrong wall.

We should have this principle of UCOP for our personal lives as well. We should use this principle with our children and wife as well. We generally take them for granted thinking that whatever we are doing, running around for targets, is all for them anyway. This is the biggest myth. Maybe we are fooling ourselves with this argument. Our family needs our time more than anything else. So we have to find ways of earning enough money and success to keep the family happy but in the pursuit of money and success, in the pursuit of things which money can buy, we should not lose the most precious things of all— the smile of your child, your spouse's happiness, your parent's time—which money can never buy.

Balance both and apply the UCOP principle to improve your personal, professional, financial and spiritual life.

❑❑❑

12

" Growth Parameters "

Reliance Industries Ltd (RIL) is one of the biggest corporations in India and mark my words, they will be THE biggest corporate group on planet Earth in the years to come. One of the reasons for this audacious prediction of mine, stems from the tagline they use, which is—"Growth is Life".

How true this is. Life is like riding a cycle; either you move forward or peddle backwards but you definitely can't stand still. No prizes for guessing what happens if you do that—you fall.

Most people sleepwalk through life. They live from one Sunday to the next because that's the day when they are not answerable to anyone (though some people have an eternal boss at home; their bitter, oops sorry, better half) and can laze around. You deserve the lazing around on Sunday only if you have slogged your backside and grey cells off during the remaining six days of the week or you are as good as a thief (a kamchor is also a chor. Not doing your job at office is as good as stealing time, which we have voluntarily given to the company in return for a good pay check) who is enjoying a holiday even though he is actually taking a holiday from his work all through the week.

Nature teaches us growth at every step. Since the time we are born to the time we breathe our last, our bodies are changing, growing, ageing and then vanishing, only to go into our next birth and start the process once again (which is the belief of Hindus).

It is said that we begin every year with a brand new body. We get a new liver every six months, a new stomach lining every five days and new skin every month. So just to digress a bit, when we say, *"I am this"* who are we referring to? Who is this *"I"*? We are referring to our body. However when our whole body gets replaced year after year then where are we really? The old "you" is gone and a new "you" has taken its place? What is the name of this new body? Is it the same? Such questions are complex but they really make you think. Actually when we say *"I am XYZ,"* we are referring to our soul which resides within us. When we say, "this is my hand" or *"this is my leg"* we speak of a physical manifestation of something that is uniquely our own. This *"my"* is what I mean when I talk about our soul. When we die, our bodies are called bodies and not by the name of the deceased, right?

The blood in our veins is constantly flowing. If you stop the flow of blood to some part of our body that part becomes useless and becomes a liability, which needs to be amputated to save the rest of the body.

Money is also called "currency". The word currency is derived from the Latin word "currens", which means *"to run"*. Its meaning was extended by the philosopher and educationist John Locke in 1699 when he used it to describe the *"circulation of money"*. Just as the working condition of the various parts of our body determines how healthy we are, which cannot happen without the circulation of blood through all the parts, money also needs to move from one hand to the next and so on, so forth. This phenomenon of money moving from through a series of hands can also be described as "the running of money", which is probably why Locke described money as currency.

Hence we should think of growth at every step and with every breath.

RIL Growth: Market potential does not determine self-potential

When RIL plans growth parameters for the year to come, they set aggressive figures as their targets, which sometimes is totally disconnected with their performance in the previous year. Most companies decide their targets for the next year based on their achievements in the previous year, but not RIL. They decide next year's target based on the potential of the market. If the market has concluded business worth Rs 1,000 and I have made Rs 100 on the market in the previous year, then ordinarily I would decide to achieve maybe Rs 120, Rs 130 or Rs 150 this year but RIL would decide to make Rs 500 (even if their last year's business was Rs 100) because they are looking at the potential of the market and not limiting themselves to its current performance.

Most of the employees in any organization are hired on the basis of their potential but their performance usually doesn't match that potential and for this the employer is to blame.

First and foremost, an employer should have the knack of selecting the right candidate for the right job. When the selection is done, the employer should make sure that his employee is given the right kind of support and encouragement to perform his duties at an optimal level.

One requires two things to be successful in a job. The first is "domain knowledge". An employer should make sure that the "domain knowledge" is downloaded to the employee in the right manner. The most important thing, even more than the download is that the employer should make sure that the employee has got all his doubts cleared in his brain before he starts his job. Consider the word "communication"; it is not just about telling something to someone. It is about telling something to someone and also making sure that the receiving party has understood what was intended by the messenger, in the proper context and that the outcome of the message is what the sender wanted to achieve.

Consider the following sentence: "This is not my sister's purse". One can attach various meanings to the same line depending on which word we lay stress on. If we lay stress on *"this"*, the object, in this case, the purse, is being given emphasis. However, if we lay stress on "my", the implicit meaning of the sentence changes. The emphasis is now on the you. So while this purse is not *"my sister's"* purse it could be someone else's sister's purse. If we lay stress on *"sisters"*, we are implying that the purse could be our mother's or wife's but not our sister's.

Any communication can potentially have several layers of meaning and hence the sender's message may not reach the receiver in the same context as intended and hence it has to be clarified and cross checked with the receiver to prevent misunderstandings.

In a scene from the movie "Double Dhamaal" starring Sanjay Dutt, Arshad Warsi, Kangana Ranaut and Mallika Sherawat, Mallika says the following dialogue to Sanju baba, she says "Mere pyar mein kabhi kami na aaye". This means that there should never be any shortage in my love for you. But she twists the dialogue slightly and an entirely new meaning emerges from this innocuous piece of dialogue. She says, *"Mere pyar mein kabhi kamina aaye"*. She's basically asking to fall in love with a scoundrel. This intelligent play of dialogue ends up delivering an entirely different message to poor Sanjay Dutt. Even the name of the character played by Mallika is "Kamini" which is again open to two different meanings, which are entirely divorced from one another.

Boot Polish Deewar: Yeh Ladka Zaroor Kuch Banega

One scene from "Deewar" that left a lasting impression on me was the scene where the child who grows up to become Amitabh has the courage to demand respect from two rich and powerful men. I have described this scene in detail in my chapter on getting an appointment with an HNI client. The small child, who is wearing a torn shirt takes offence when his two rich clients toss a coin at him instead of giving it to him in his hand. Such an attitude is very important or I dare say, of primary importance if someone wants to grow in life. In the film, the attitude displayed by the child impresses one of the men (played by veteran actor "Iftekhar") and he tells his companion (played by "Sudhir;" the man portrayed as a habitual rapist along with actor Ranjeet in many films made in the 70s) that this kid will not do a boot polish all his life. He says *"Jis din iss ladke ne speed pakdi, yeh sabko peeche chod jayega"*. This translates to: the moment he catches speed (growth opportunity) in life, he will move far ahead of the others. The main reason for Iftekhar's statement was that against all odds—being only eight-years-old, broke, and fatherless and a pavement dweller—the child has immense respect for himself. Hence it hurt the child when coins were flung at him. I would say, this quality of respecting oneself, respecting one's performance in corporate life is a major quality when one talks of growth in the corporate world.

The definition of "attitude" for me is to not care about what the world thinks and to believe in one's self; to achieve honest, unbelievable and aggressive feats, unmindful of the repercussions of one's actions. To possess a devil-may-care attitude and have the courage to take risks.

People who achieve great deeds already have the seed of success or the potential to grow, in them. Somewhere along the way they get an opportunity or most of the time they convert problems into opportunities, overcome them and grow.

Opportunities have the unique habit of coming disguised as problems. Smart people recognize this and jump on them with relish. Success comes only when opportunity meets preparation. Successful men are prepared for every eventuality and anticipate trouble before it takes place. They know how to completely cash in on opportunities and grow to a higher level. Foolish men complain of noise when opportunity knocks on their door.

Deewar: Yahan meri maa bhi eetein uthatee thi

In Deewar, Amitabh buys a high-rise apartment from a shrewd businessman. After the papers are signed and the deal goes through, the shrewd businessman needles Amitabh by saying

"Maaf karna, Vijaysaab, aapko dhandha karna nahi aata. Aap yeh building mehengi le gaye. Agar aap kahte, toh shayad mein ek do lakh aur kam deta." (I would have reduced prize by 1 or 2 Lakhs)

On hearing this Amitabh says,

"Dhandha toh aapko karna nahi aata. Agar aap ne mujhse, iss building ke 10 lakh rupee bhi aur maange hote, toh main de deta". (I would have paid Rs. 10 L more)

Now it is the turn of the businessman to get confused. He seems worried because he is wondering how he lost out on the extra money. He asks,

"Achcha? Aisi kya baat hai is building mein"? (What is so special about this building?)

Amitabh looks at the building, and one can see it being reflected in his sunglasses as he says,

"Aaj se 20 saal pahle jab yeh building ban rahi thi, tab meri ma ne yahan eetein uthaee thee aur aaj mein yeh building apni maa ko tohfe mein dene jaa raha hoon". (My mother had worked as a labourer during the construction of this building and today I am going to gift it to her.)

This, in my books, is growth. The woman who was working at the site when that building was made, is getting the same building as gift from her own son. Awesome!

Stay at the top or vanish

Today in corporate life, you have to run faster to stay exactly where you are. And you have to sprint like Usain Bolt to march ahead of all the others. This reminds me of a story:

A lion was chasing two friends. As they ran for their lives, one of them says to the other that he is not trying to outrun the lion but trying to outrun him because the lion is going to catch the one running slowly, while giving the other guy time to escape. The lion could have killed either of the two but he only needs one to satisfy his hunger so the one who is left, survives to see another day.

The above example is applicable in today's corporate jungle. We are always competing against someone. Ideally one should compete with oneself to achieve what one is capable of. Success is realising your maximum potential.

A tiger takes a few steps back in order to pounce on you

In the film "Baazigar" Shah Rukh Khan wants to impress Kajol so he gets into a car race with her father. Even though he could have won the race effortlessly, at the very last moment he takes his foot off the accelerator and allows Kajol's dad to win. When they meet, her father asks him why he lost the race on purpose, to which he says,

"Kabhi kabhi jeetne ke liye, haarna bhi padta hai. Haar kar jeetne wale ko Baazigar kahte hain." (Sometimes you have to accept smaller defeats to get bigger success.)

This is true everywhere. Sometimes you have to take a few steps backwards, prepare and come back charging and achieve much more than what you could have if you had continued along the same path without stopping to think about your plan of action.

Growth by hook or crook?

Most people believe in growing by hook or by crook; mostly by crook. This kind of growth is short-lived. Growth should give you inner satisfaction and happiness and this will come only after you have been fair in your dealings with others. It is better not to get the honor yet deserve it than to get honored without deserving it. We may lie to the world but our inner voice will always prick our conscience.

When you win fairly, you grow in values, conduct and character. These are important ingredients for happiness.

Degrowth: RD Burman, Dev Anand, Rajesh Khanna

You have to keep pace with the changes around you and change (grow) accordingly. Running water doesn't stink.

Dev Anand refused to accept his surroundings and the changes taking place all around him. He refused to grow. As a result he faced monumental failures in the later part of his career, yet he remained adamant that what he was doing was right. If only any one of his later movies had been a hit he would have made a strong come back. However he refused to be in step with the new world and paid the price for his stubbornness.

Yash Chopra on the other hand, grew with the generation. Can you imagine that the man who made his first movie "Dhool ka Phool" around five decades ago in black and white, also made "Veer Zaara "starring Shah Rukh Khan and Preeti Zinta and Rani Mukherjee?

If you don't change, the world will change you and that hurts. Self-change is bearable but forced change is traumatic. When an egg is broken from the inside, it signals the arrival of new life. But try breaking an egg from the outside. It is not of much use, that is, unless you're making an omelette.

Adi Chopra, the son of Yash Chopra very wisely has shifted (and thus grown) his lens to making movies with exciting new directors. Now from being a director, he has become a mentor to many and under his leadership the Yash Raj banner has scaled new heights of success, wealth, fame and reputation. Hats off to him! He is focusing only on movies and not on useless things (as far as the craft of movie making goes) like interviews, game shows, etc. He is sensible and focused. Focus is not about saying "yes" to one thing, it is also about saying "no" to 99 other things. With focus anyone can get anything he wants in life.

Dhirubhai: Phone call less than cost of post card

Growth also requires you to have big heart and a big vision. Dhirubhai, the father of Dhiruism used to say that *"People see things and say why? Whereas I don't see anything and I say why not?"*

When an incoming call cost Rs 16 per minute (This was on August 15, 1995, when mobile phones entered India), it was Dhirubhai's vision to make the call cheaper than a post card.

He and his sons achieved this vision.

Many people think Dhirubhai employed crooked means to achieve his goals. What they say may be true but we should never forget that he had the welfare of poor people in mind when he took up any project. He always wanted their upliftment. His cheap call rates helped many poor people earn a livelihood.

In the process of enriching the poor, a person who succeeds in enriching others will be rich himself as was the case with Dhirubhai. His was the only company to make good quality fabric available to the poor at reasonable rates. For achieving this end, he may have manipulated many people along the way. But if you have read the Mahabharata, you realise that Lord Krishna did exactly the same thing. He could not have won the war without manipulation and cheating (albeit for a good cause). Since his objective was good, we accepted his path of deceit. Lord Krishna would not have been able to kill Dronacharya, Bhishma, Karna and Duryodhan, among others, without outwitting or cheating them.

In the same way, Dhirubhai could not have uplifted the poor without bribing a lot of politicians.

Dhirubhai broke the system to help the people who were supposed to benefit through the same system and who were getting exploited by the same system.

I have immense admiration for Dhirubhai Ambani. If we have even two more Dhurubhais today, we would be able to wipe out the U.S.A. from their top spot in the world.

I can give you an example from Bollywood as well. Take actor Akshay Kumar's (AK) change of track from action to comedy. AK realized that if he wanted to grow, he had to adapt to a new genre of acting and embrace comedy roles instead of sticking to action films. He went on to make films like Hera Pheri, Singh is King and Welcome, which were big box office hits. He made the transition from action to comedy seamlessly and now he is amongst the top stars, alongside the Khans and Hrithik Roshan, in terms of popularity.

Stick to one thing for growth: Should you dig one 10 feet (ft.) deep hole to find oil or dig 2ft deep holes at five different places?

Focus is required for growth. If you are told that you have to dig a hole of 10ft to get oil, what will you do? Most people dig shallow 2ft deep holes at five different places, which amounts to a total of 10ft and get nothing for their efforts because their focus was off. The one who digs a 10ft hole at one place, will get the oil.

Actor Govinda used to sign multiple films and used to hope that somehow one of them will hit the jackpot. He was not focused on a single film and lacked the understanding required to recognise a good script. Thus even though he is extremely talented, he got stuck selling hair oil in telesales advertisements that only appear on late night television (though he has made a comeback through films like Kill-Dil and Happy Ending). An actor who is far less talented than him but a lot more focused, namely Anil Kapoor, is now working even in Hollywood productions.

In the film "Deewana Mastana" directed by David Dhawan,

Govinda was pitted against Anil Kapoor but Anil was given a side kick—Johnny Lever—who is a very popular actor. This reveals that at that point, the director equated Govinda with Anil plus Johnny.

This same Govinda is now cooling his heels at home. This is reverse growth.

Follow the above principles and go higher up in the corporate world without ever having to go into reverse gear, like the talented Govinda.

Growth and only growth is life!

❑❑❑

www.ingramcontent.com/pod-product-compliance
Lightning Source LLC
Chambersburg PA
CBHW021930190326
41519CB00009B/967